Wilton Barnhardt's brilliant, hilarious, outspoken introduction gives us a good idea of the origrinality ahead in this eclectic collection of highly personal writing. Describing Oakwood Cemetery, he writes, "Here you see the nineteenth-century cult of the Confederate cause with an overlay of good ol' Victorian death-obsession. . . . This is the cemetery where Elizabeth Edwards came for daily communion with her son, Wade; this is where Lorenzo Charles is buried near Jim Valvano, principals of the ultimate Cinderella-team NCAA basketball championship for N.C. State in 1983 . . . but there are Confederate heroes aplenty, and white supremacist governors and staunch segregationists. . . . I never wander through Oakwood without being mightily glad that some of these men and their ruinous philosophies are six feet under the dirt where they belong." Again and again we find the past and the present nestled cheek to cheek, if not always dancing.

. . . In an act of homage to her Aunt Bernice, Tracie Fellers tries on the dress she once wore to the black debutante ball. Tom Hawkins pays a poetic visit to the state fairgrounds at every stage of his life. Cameroon-born Juliana M. Nfah-Abbenyi negotiates her way through a difficult immigration experience before finding "home" in Raleigh . . . Betty Adcock writes about Reedy Creek Park, "a forest in the middle of Raleigh" . . .

The old beloved Balentine's Cafeteria remembered by Dana Wynne Lindquist is bookended by Ashley Christensen's hot new Poole's Diner, described by Andrea Wiegl. In "Hungry," Angela Davis-Gardner's fictional narrator is literally starving for the past. The daughter in Hillary Hebert's "Ladies of the Marble Hearth" has a very tough time pulling off the 420th luncheon meeting of her mother's book club. Rich fare indeed, and much food for thought can be found throughout this collection, a banquet for the senses and the intellect alike.

—LEE SMITH, author, *Fair and Tender Ladies*

The greatest pleasure of my bookselling career has been discovering, reading, and promoting the works of North Carolina writers, and a great many of them, as you'll learn in this excellent collection, live or work in Raleigh. It was obvious from the beginning that our customers were as enamored as I of their fine writing, both fiction and nonfiction.

This is a book to be savored—let it guide you into a rich panoply of nationally and internationally known Raleigh writers.

—NANCY OLSON, Quail Ridge Books

27 VIEWS OF RALEIGH

outside the beltline

N.C. Museum of Art ←

St. Augustine's →

STATE CAPITOL

SiR, WALTER Raleigh

→ Beach

N.C. State

MEMORIAL BELLTOWER

PULLEN PARK CAROUSEL

ACORN
IN
MOORE SQUARE

↓
SHAW UNIVERSITY

27 VIEWS
OF
RALEiGH

The City of Oaks in Prose & Poetry

Introduction by Wilton Barnhardt

27 Views of Raleigh: The City of Oaks in Prose and Poetry
Introduction by Wilton Barnhardt
© Eno Publishers, 2013

Each selection herein is the copyrighted property of its respective
author or publisher, if so noted on the Permissions page, and appears in
this volume by arrangement with the individual writer or publisher.

Eno Publishers
P.O. Box 158
Hillsborough, North Carolina 27278
www.enopublishers.org

ISBN-13: 978-0-9832475-5-5
ISBN-10: 0-9832475-5-2
Library of Congress Control Number: 2013938532
10 9 8 7 6 5 4 3 2 1

Cover illustration by Daniel Wallace, Chapel Hill, North Carolina
Design and typesetting by Horse & Buggy Press, Durham, North Carolina

Publisher's Acknowledgments

A huge thank you to Wilton Barnhardt and our twenty-eight writers who
have created a literary montage of Raleigh, now and then. Thanks also to Jill
McCorkle, Lee Smith, and Nancy Olson—Raleigh's legendary bookseller
at Quail Ridge Books—who all contributed many great suggestions as Eno
compiled this collection.

The publisher also wishes to thank Gita Schonfeld, Adrienne Fox, and Virginia
Smith for their careful editorial work on the views. Thanks also to our indefatigable
interns Jeramie Orton, Kelsi Oliver, and Kendell Richmond, and to Daniel Wallace
for his colorful rendering of the City of Oaks.

www.ncarts.org

Eno Publishers appreciates the generous support of the North
Carolina Arts Council whose grant helped fund the publishing
of 27 *Views of Raleigh*.

Acknowledgments & Permissions

Some of the 27 *Views of Raleigh* have appeared in whole or in part in other publications:

"The Parade," by Jimmy Creech, is adapted from *Adam's Gift*, published by Duke University Press. All rights reserved. Republished by permission of Duke University Press.

David Rigsbee's poem "North State" was published in his book, *School of the Americas*, and also appeared in *AGNI* (Fall 2011).

A version of Lenard D. Moore's poem "Raleigh Jazz Festival, 1986" originally appeared in *Black American Literature Forum* (Fall 1987), now known as the *African American Review*.

Hillary Hebert's short story "Ladies of the Marble Hearth" was first published in *New Stories from the American South: The Year's Best 1995* (Algonquin Books).

Margaret Maron's view, "The Carousel at Pullen Park," is excerpted from her novel *Bootlegger's Daughter: A Deborah Knott Mystery* (Mysterious Press, 1992).

"A Force of Nature," by Andrea Weigl, is adapted from an article of the same title that first appeared in the *News & Observer* (February 20, 2011).

"Where the Beauty Lies," by Liza Roberts, is adapted from an article that first appeared in *Walter* (2013).

George Kessel's short story "George Delivers the Goods" is adapted from his novel *Good News from Outer Space*, which has recently been re-released as an ebook with a new introduction.

Table of Contents

STREET SCENES

CLOSE-UPS

VIEWS FROM BEFORE

VIEWS IN FICTION

Preface

27 VIEWS OF RALEIGH is a literary montage and an understatement—readers will find twenty-eight perspectives of life in North Carolina's City of Oaks, plus an insightful and jocular introduction by novelist Wilton Barnhardt. But even twenty-eight plus one barely skim the surface of life and its complexities in Joel Lane's dream settlement.

27 *Views of Raleigh* is not a guide in any traditional sense. It is more a composite created from a variety of genres—fiction, essays, poems. The views span genres, neighborhoods, decades and generations, racial and cultural experiences, perspectives of born-and-raised Raleighites and transplants, to create a distinct sense of place. Some of the views herein celebrate the city and its people, present and past; others expose its fissures, of family and history, of politics and history, of race and history. Some shine a lens on a place or a person evolving; some focus on the imperative of change; some zero in on an environment changed and unchanged. And one view imagines a science-fictionalized Raleigh.

It also reveals a fact about the city not widely known outside its Inside/Outside-the-Beltline world: Raleigh boasts a fine and well-populated community of writers, a quasi-secret that is no longer safe.

Eno hopes that 27 *Views of Raleigh* provides readers with both a sense of recognition and one of discovery, as they delve into how twenty-seven (plus two) of its inhabitants think about the place they call home.

Elizabeth Woodman

Eno Publishers | Spring 2013

Introduction

RALEIGH ALMOST DIDN'T EXIST twice in its history, and I don't mean thanks to tornadoes or hurricanes, though weather—Hurricane Hazel, Hurricane Fran—has had a deadly go at our city a time or two.

The first existential crisis concerned whether the city should be here at all.

The colonial Assembly had met at Edenton, then at New Bern, where British Governor William Tryon had built himself a lavish residence and "capitol," mocked by the people as "Tryon Palace," although the name was to stick. Once the American Revolution was afoot, it was thought more prudent to move the capital inland so the British navy wouldn't so easily come calling. Much of the state's court business had been in Hillsborough for years, and so the legislature moved there. Hillsboroughans a few years earlier had erupted over the taxes that built Tryon Palace, dishonest sheriffs, and pretty much any taxes anywhere; they led the charge in the Regulator Rebellion. Governor Tryon had quashed the uprising, then hanged six of the ringleaders in Hillsborough on a hastily constructed gallows, paying for the war against the Regulators . . . by raising taxes. After the Revolutionary War, the locals persisted in antifederalism, not liking the sound of the new-fangled U.S. Constitution. Those Hillsborough folk really didn't like to be told what to do. Maybe a more neutral capital was needed.

A wealthy planter, Joel Lane, holder of a thousand acres of what became downtown Raleigh, convinced the young government to buy his land and raise a new utopian capital city much like Washington, DC, free of influential first families and established corruptions. (So much for that dream.) Lane was magnificently adept in schmoozing authorities. Once upon a time, the Raleigh we love today was entirely in Johnston County. I think I speak for all current residents in thanking Joel Lane for carving out a new county years before the American Revolution and getting his personal fiefdom approved by Governor Tryon. He disarmingly proposed it be named after the governor's wife, Margaret Wake. Joel Lane's house, circa 1760s, still stands, the oldest dwelling in Raleigh, and if you're a schoolchild you have been force-marched through the dwelling on an educational daytrip.

There was a 1792 capitol, which was enlarged in the 1820s, and this really was the pride of the state. In the most spendthrift gesture since Governor Tryon and his palace, the legislature decided to invest in High Art. The legislature asked Thomas Jefferson's advice and he recommended Antonio Canova, the neoclassical sculptor, famous throughout Europe. His work was prohibitively pricey but for once—maybe the only time— the legislature said money is no object, even when the cost exceeded $10,000 for his statue of George Washington. Canova was then the reigning sculptor in the world; you can see his "Three Graces" in the Hermitage, his "Psyche Revived by Cupid's Kiss" in the Louvre, his papal tombs in Rome. Added to these points of pilgrimage . . . Raleigh, North Carolina. Canova's statue of Washington, enrobed like a Roman general, sat in the rotunda. It was so darn valuable that people began to fear for it. What if the roof fell in? Someone proposed putting the statue on rollers so it could be whisked away if the rafters came down; that was overruled for being too tacky. What about the smoky fireplaces and the sooty chimneys . . . could something be done to fireproof the capitol? In what seems a metaphorical moment for North Carolina and its government, in attempting to fireproof the capitol in 1831, the workers accidentally burned it to the ground and the priceless Canova was destroyed. Should have gone with the rollers.

The second time Raleigh almost disappeared concerned Union General William Tecumseh Sherman who was, one must admit, good at making towns disappear.

Confederate General Joseph E. Johnston had been extravagantly retreating across the South, backing up from Georgia to North Carolina, and failing to stop Sherman at any point. General Robert E. Lee had already surrendered at Appomattox as this last ragtag gasp of Confederate glory made its way up (what would be) I-95 toward Raleigh. There was one perfectly sorry battle at Bentonville where, for once, offense-challenged Johnston looked to surprise and better Sherman . . . but, of course, Sherman had superior numbers. Johnston withdrew to Raleigh, and when that was untenable, to Greensboro where he spent the remaining days of his command trying to persuade Confederate President Jefferson Davis (a man he disliked even more than he did Sherman) that the jig was up. Sherman made himself comfortable in the governor's mansion (long gone, where Memorial Auditorium is now) and toasted the defeat of the South at a party at Haywood House (still standing, on Blount Street).

While Sherman was in town (and most everyone else including Governor Zebulon Vance had scampered off), news reached him that President Lincoln had been assassinated. Predictably, his officers and soldiers yearned to raze Raleigh to ashes, just as they'd expertly done to Atlanta and Columbia. Sherman issued orders that nothing should be done to any property or any person and disobedience would meet with the strictest punishments . . . and Raleigh was spared. Sherman knew that North Carolina was the most reluctant of the Rebel states; the local newspaper had excoriated President Davis for years, and there had been a political faction, led by future-governor William Woods Holden, who wished to sue for early peace. Mr. Sherman is still disliked in the South for his scorched-earth antics, but it seems some mention should be due to him for not burning down Raleigh when he had the chance and few Northerners would have blamed him.

After the war, Raleigh became known for its cemeteries. We have several national and state cemeteries teeming with an immense number of Civil War dead. The Confederate hospitals were based here and usually admission to a clinic bed was a one-way trip. With the railroads torn up, many rebel soldiers could not have their bodies shipped back home to points south, so they were buried here. Oakwood Cemetery is an underrated if somewhat morbid tourist attraction. Here you see the nineteenth-century cult of the Confederate cause with an overlay of good ol' Victorian death-obsession. Stone cherubs, angels racked with grief, granite urns, and crowns of laurel atilt on downcast statues of youths in Hellenic robes. . . . This is the cemetery where Elizabeth Edwards came for daily communion with her late son, Wade; this is where Lorenzo Charles is buried near Jim Valvano, principals of the ultimate Cinderella-team NCAA basketball championship for N.C. State in 1983. But there are Confederate heroes aplenty, and white supremacist governors (Charles Aycock) and staunch segregationists (Senator Jesse Helms) buried here, and "heroes" like Lieutenant Walsh—the one man to get off a potshot at Sherman when the Union soldiers peacefully took the town—who was hanged for his gesture in Burke Square. People still festoon his grave with flowers and tributes. I never wander through Oakwood without being mightily glad that some of these men and their ruinous philosophies are six feet under the dirt where they belong.

President Andrew Johnson, Raleigh's rarely claimed favorite son, succeeded Lincoln and appointed William Woods Holden to the governorship. Holden would win it in his own right and spend most of his time fighting the Ku Klux Klan. No Southern governor ever made the Klan's destruction more of a priority, and for this and other offenses he was impeached and removed, the first state governor to be so treated in

U.S. history. (His pal Johnson, with far more reason, was impeached as well—you'll note the nation has not rushed back to North Carolina for a president since.)

During Reconstruction you can see some bright spots—the founding of Shaw College, the first black university in the United States in 1865, and then Saint Augustine's College, two years later. But progress and good news were in short supply through Reconstruction and the Jim Crow era. After the civic coup in Wilmington in 1898, the cry of "Black Disenfranchisement" became the slogan of Democratic governors. By 1908 no black vote was counted in North Carolina. Raleigh's history from the Civil War to the civil rights era is the story of the South, and that's an epic story that even now—I refer you to the recent (nationally embarrassing) Wake County School Board fights where race was front and center—hasn't found that happy concluding chapter quite yet.

So why is Raleigh in the twenty-first century such a good place to live? Bloomberg, MSNBC, *Businessweek,* the Milken Institute, the American Institute for Economic Research, Kiplinger—all showing their love, recommending Raleigh in their Top Ten Places to Live, with frequent appearances at the Number One spot. More people are coming than going—this is the fourth fastest-growing city in the United States. In 1990 there were 212,000 people here; now there are 416,000. Yep, that's a 100 percent gain in roughly two decades, and the crowding of schools and thoroughfares shows it.

For all that, Raleigh is a well-run city and wins awards for civic planning. Development, though not always careful, has bestowed "the City of Oaks" with parks and trails and greenways, and many old neighborhoods seem more forest than city, for those inclined to stroll. It is a high-tech corridor and leg of the famous Research Triangle. The five in-town universities lie thick on the ground, and this area has more bachelor degree–holding people per capita than anywhere in the country (or some lists have us as Number 2, behind Seattle). We have a thriving downtown that doesn't close up at five p.m.—just the opposite. There is an exciting, trendy restaurant culture, a hockey team that won the Stanley Cup, the best independent bookstore in the South (Quail Ridge Books), a well-regarded ballet and symphony, the impressively good North Carolina Museum of Art that rivals any collection outside of the nation's major cities. We have four gay bars. We have the best farmers' market in the state (or, if you trust my European visitors whom I take there, the best produce market on this side of the Atlantic). The Triangle is the epicenter of college basketball (sorry Indiana, sorry Kentucky—come back to me when you have three regularly ranked teams less than twenty miles from each other). In the thirty-year block, 1982–2012, *nine* of the NCAA Men's Basketball championships have been claimed by one of the Triangle schools, almost a third of the victories. Case closed. Raleigh is two hours from the beach and three to four from the Blue Ridge Mountains; Raleigh straddles the Piedmont (where the barbecue is slow-cooked pork shoulder) and the Coastal Plain, "Down East" (where the sauce is vinegar and spices, and the pig is pit-cooked in its entirety). And we keep winning awards for Friendliest City, Best City for Singles, most "Family Friendly," all of that.

And I love Raleigh, too. As do scores of musicians, writers, artists, chefs, and other creative types, some of whom you are about to read in *27 Views of Raleigh: The City of Oaks in Prose & Poetry*.

Yes, it would help if the rest of the state didn't keep sending simpletons to the legislature, but I suppose that is the burden of being a state capital. Happily, it gives us something to complain and roll our eyes about. We seem to have flourished not because we solved all the problems of the New South, despite leading the way now and again, but because we the citizens of Raleigh decided to be erudite, cultured, enriched, and entertained in spite of the government of North Carolina's stumbles, from the Republican state senator trying to criminalize the exposure of breasts in 2013 to the long and astounding history of graft in the once-entrenched Democratic party, where, with Illinoisan frequency, jail time and indictments often await our departing governors and legislators. The capital's shenanigans, its self-parodic lunacies, make for headlines and outrages but from a world brought to us by out-of-towners, temporary elected types confined to a few blocks of downtown we don't much run into. The rest of us Raleighites are busy getting on with a really comfortable, enjoyable life.

Wilton Barnhardt
Raleigh, North Carolina | Spring 2013

WILTON BARNHARDT was born in Winston-Salem, North Carolina, and now lives in Raleigh, where he teaches in the Master of Fine Arts in Creative Writing program at North Carolina State University. He is a former reporter for *Sports Illustrated* (his beat: NASCAR), and is also the author of four novels, including *Emma Who Saved My Life* and *Lookaway, Lookaway*.

A Place Called Home

On the Corner

GRAYSON HAVER CURRIN

I MEAN NO DISRESPECT, but I never wanted to live in Oakwood.

At least from the outside, Raleigh's first historic neighborhood suggested the sort of genuflection that had always made me uncomfortable. "*Oak*-wood," people would say, overemphasizing that first syllable as though the name alone were sacrament. And in a way, it was: Full of stately old homes and veritable mansions, wealthy denizens and city leaders, Oakwood long seemed to me a power hold in this growing city, a place where important folks went to roost with their kin.

People in Oakwood had specialized purple porch flags emblazoned with the neighborhood name, as though passersby didn't already know. People in Oakwood had raised-letter door plaques on their front porches, faithfully telling the interlopers when their historic parcel had been erected. People in Oakwood had buckets of disposable income to spend on Christmas decorations, a lesson learned every time one traveled its hallowed streets after Thanksgiving. So I was pretty sure I wasn't meant to be one of the People in Oakwood.

In the spring of 2012, however, we needed a new home. Tina and I had been dating for the better part of two years and living together for most of that time. After our first six obsessive months together, her Durham roommate had packed his bags and boxes in the dead of night, splitting just before Christmas while we visited Tina's family a dozen hours away. When we returned on Christmas Eve, the door was open, the house was freezing, and her hungry, confused cats were outside, waiting for mom. On New Year's Eve, we sat together in a coffee shop, filling out a lease application and asking the questions that naive new romantics unexpectedly entering into domesticity tend to have: What's your social security number? And your driver's license number? And you've never been evicted, *right*?

Less than two weeks later, we'd largely settled into a small, square brick rental in Raleigh's Longview neighborhood, a long walk or circuitous bike ride from downtown. We loved the little nest—its screened-in front porch, its large backyard, its relative quiet. For the first six months, we even spoke of buying it one day, so long as our sincerely good-old-boy landlord, Roy, would let it go to two lefty kids in love.

With the arrival of summer, that dream died slowly, like winter pansies wilting as the season slips past: We adopted a second dog, a hulking and handsome pit bull named Boris, who came to own the porch. We started cooking more, which turned the already-cramped kitchen into a claustrophobe's nightmare. And as the days warmed and as daylight stretched further into the evening, foot traffic from all directions increased. Kids skipping out of a nearby school stood on the sidewalk to bicker or joke or just waste the day. Boris, a magnificent alarm system without much of a false-alarm filter, barked incessantly.

One evening, at Boris's continued urging, I walked outside to see what was the matter. A young man and woman were walking by, trapped in the throes of a lover's quarrel. The man huffed and hollered, flinging his arms in paroxysms of frustration. When he reached our neighbor's house, he stopped, took a swing at the mailbox and sent it flying from its post. After he'd passed, I stepped outside and reaffixed the aluminum cylinder, hoping that our elderly neighbor would never realize the foul.

Later that night, as we slept with our windows wide open, three shots from a pistol broke the still of our sleep. The cops came, shining their flashlights in the yard for discharged cases and footprints. Sometime just before dawn, Boris finally curled back into a ball and went to sleep.

That was one of several such incidents—not the last, not the first, but certainly the clarion call that maybe it was time to start searching for something else. Months later, a few kids died a block away, an incident barely mentioned by the news media. Tina kept her eye on the city's crime map, emailing me most mornings with robberies and shootings and rapes that had happened within earshot.

Then, one night, after returning home from a late concert, an officer stopped us a few hundred yards short of our driveway, telling us we couldn't go home yet. They'd closed that section of town, he'd said, pretending that other details just didn't exist. So we sat for two hours in a pizza parlor's parking lot, listening for tidbits through a cell phone's police scanner application. On the radio, we could hear Boris barking as police discussed how best to disarm our neighbor, ostensibly holding his family hostage inside their new rental with the bright red door. When we finally made it home, we saw that the SWAT team had set up its headquarters on our front lawn. Boris slept inside that night.

That was enough. The house-hunt, previously something of a sideline weekend hobby with a few leads that went cold, suddenly became urgent. Tina turned into a real-estate sleuth, checking multiple sites multiple times a day, looking for something two twenty-somethings with mixed credit (hers platinum, mine polyester) might afford. We called real estate agents, lined up a few meetings and even made an offer that went unaccepted.

And so Oakwood was reconsidered. In the race to get away, my consistent refrain—"I really don't want to live in Oakwood"—seemed too stubborn for our little family's good. Raleigh's first historic neighborhood became part of our targeted market. A five-minute walk from downtown's developing epicenter, it tends to do that to young couples who spend most of their time, money, and weekends in the city center.

But it seemed at first a moot concession: Most of the homes for sale in Oakwood were well beyond our financial reach, a fact that churned our stomachs when we plugged the specifics of one $500,000 beauty into an online mortgage calculator. That was more than okay with me, a kid who grew up on his family's farm in rural North Carolina and with a father who often called the trappings of the rich "vulgar displays of wealth." Oakwood's towering Second Empires, massive Victorians, and sprawling plantation lawns hinted at some latent Confederate vitality. As the prodigal progressive grandson of a South Carolina woman who still refers to her black gardener as "June Bug" and to many of her neighbors as "colored," old Southern glory has made me squirm since I was old enough to know better. Oakwood, I reckoned, could keep its *Yard of the Month* sign.

There was that *one* house on the corner, though. On a beautiful Sunday afternoon, we visited our first home in Oakwood, a modest place at the intersection of one of the city's busiest thoroughfares, Edenton Street, and one of the neighborhood's many parallel cross streets. It had a massive backyard with a gazebo and a fence, ancient pine floors that showed their age with their slopes, and tiny twin front porches that dated to its run as a duplex. There were built-in bookshelves, a large kitchen with strangely vaulted ceilings, *four fireplaces*—it was something like the house we'd both imagined.

Thing is, we still couldn't afford it, no matter how much we tried to adjust the numbers or consider renting out one room. So we waited and saw other places but, all along, kept our eyes on the price of the house that sat like daily bait on both of our paths to work. One morning, Tina called to say that the price had dropped yet again and that it *might* be within our range. We called the agent, who'd long ago rightly dismissed us as kids who couldn't afford Oakwood; by the weekend, we'd made an offer, and by the end of the weekend, it had been accepted. I was elated, even if it meant that I'd be living in Oakwood.

During the last seven months, I've fallen in love with the house. I'm excited to get home every evening, a little bit miffed to leave every morning.

And I've realized that most everything the real estate agent promised we'd adore about this place was correct—from the hidden storage compartments scattered throughout to the deck that overlooks Edenton Street. When we made the purchase, the agent touted the historical relevance of the home, built, she'd said, in 1920. A month after living there, though, we learned that our little parcel at the southeastern edge of Oakwood had actually been built in 1868 by a carpenter and recently freed slave, Hilliard Williams, with his wife, Julia. There were four such houses on our corner, but after the city stretched Edenton Street, only the one we now call ours remained.

But the chief selling point, I've learned, is one that no MLS fact sheet or historical record would ever list: Our property sits directly at the corner of Oakwood and the rest of the world, giving it a rare and constantly renewing multiplicity. The neighborhood itself tends to be restive and quiet; at its center, and especially at night, Oakwood can be as still as the bucolic country setting in which I was raised. But at its edge, where we are, it teems with the city's full bustle, with parents pushing strollers to museums a few blocks away and flocks of friends walking all hours of night and day toward the city's watering holes.

So on one side of our house, the Oakwood side, our neighbors occasionally fly a Tea Party flag and, true to its snake-bolstered mantra, keep to their own. In eight months, I've seen them maybe four times. But on the other side, where we sleep at night, the Number 15 bus rolls to a stop with remarkable consistency, just a few feet from our bedroom window. I've even started to recognize some of its passengers, nodding at them through the library window.

Sitting on either of those small twin porches, you can watch the property work as a crossroads. The divergent viewpoints and lifestyles of everyone in this city seem to congregate for a moment at the stoplight beside my house. For the past eight months, I've been fairly up-to-date about new hip-hop singles, as cars headed downtown on Edenton Street often blast them from open automobile windows. Each Saturday morning, guided Segway caravans bring tourists through the neighborhood and just pass us. They wave and smile politely, barely acknowledging our little lodge as they realize they've just crossed the boundary of much bigger homes. I always wonder if the people tucked beneath their shiny black helmets realize they've just passed two halfway houses and a soup kitchen on their way into opulence. From our corner, everything about this city feels very close and, therefore, somehow at a safe, observable distance.

From said vantage, I've realized that Oakwood itself isn't so bad. I still poke fun at it on a near-daily basis, laughing at the neighborhood listserv's infinite and infinitely inane discussions concerning proper methods of dog feces disposal or the neighbors who still seem to regard the bearded man and tattooed woman on the corner with suspicion. Tina generally takes these chances to remind me of my recent antipathy: "You don't want to live in Oakwood, anyway, baby," she'll say, smiling crooked.

But the fabric here is a rich community support network, the sort that a neighborhood must tend to foster when it's previously warded off encroaching highways and urban decay. In Oakwood, yard sales are inclusive and coordinated events, with multiple homes throughout the little district opening their (generally spacious) front porches and backyards to thrift prowlers. And that listserv, however sometimes petty, is one of the deepest resources I've ever found within Raleigh—if you need to borrow something, from metal chairs for a Super Bowl party to advice on handymen, you simply ask.

At the start of January, I woke up before dawn on a Monday morning to find the listserv bustling with sad activity. Details were thin, but it seemed that only hours before, two men had broken into a house to rob a family new to the neighborhood. We later learned that the husband had been shot in the spine as he tried to stop the intruders from raping his wife. Those facts didn't emerge for a few days, but Oakwood's response emerged immediately. Neighbors volunteered their time preparing meals or cleaning clothes, their advice on alarm systems, and their talents to raise funds. At the church just a few blocks from the shooting, gospel singers gathered beneath the lights of television cameras as everyone wrapped their arms around one another—acting as a community, not as a collection of very nice homes.

Tina and I had dealt with neighborhood shootings before, but we'd always had to sort out our facts and feelings in the privacy of our own home, largely in the dark about things that happened even next door. But Oakwood made it feel like our concern and our fight, even if we'd never met the new neighbors on East Lane Street.

Standing amid that swirl of song, I realized that, back in Longview, this is what we'd always been missing: People from whom we could borrow, people with whom we could worry, people beside whom we could live. People, I guess, in Oakwood.

GRAYSON HAVER CURRIN grew up outside of Fuquay-Varina, across the street from his family's farm. Apart from a wayward stint in Durham, he's lived in Raleigh since 2001, when he moved to the big city to attend North Carolina State University. He now lives in Oakwood with his wife, Tina, their dogs, Alice and Sunn, and their cat, Bastian. He is the *Independent Weekly*'s music editor and a contributor and columnist for the music website Pitchfork Media. He is co-director of the Hopscotch Music Festival. He has a beard.

In a Relationship with Raleigh: It's Complicated

PEGGY PAYNE

WE MET IN 1954 WHEN I WAS FIVE YEARS OLD and went to visit—all by myself!—my twenty-something aunt, a single girl with a job in the big city. What I remember: the sun porch at her apartment in a big old house she shared on Blount Street; the busy crowded urban feel of Fayetteville Street rushing past me; a Belk's with a cafeteria inside, which we didn't have in Wilmington; the art museum snack bar where I somehow tipped over our table and spilled Aunt Betty's coffee.

On this trip, I decided most of my future, though I hadn't realized it until now.

How it happened: While I was there, Betty got a phone call from a man who wanted her to go out with him that night (this particular man caused a ripple of excitement through the household). So two of her friends took me for a long, long sightseeing ride. The key moment for me that evening: The car entered a traffic circle, and as the entertaining gossip flowed from the front seat, I looked down a connecting avenue to see a swoop of hill and, at the end, an immense lighted castle of a church. What could this be? Duke University, offered one of the front-seat friends.

A school? Well then, this was the school for me. We were riding through Durham, but I didn't know that. It was all Raleigh to me.

Twelve years later, as a Duke freshman, I would make my next visit to Raleigh proper. Of course, I'd heard mention of the place in the intervening years. Occasionally my father would go out of town for the day; Mom would explain, "He's gone to Raleigh to get money for the college." Daddy was a trustee for Wilmington College, which was moving and growing, eventually to become UNC-W. Raleigh was where you went to get money for that.

For my second visit to the city, I was again in a back seat at night, double-dating with a boy whose girlfriend was at Peace College. Once again, I looked down a long stretch of road to the lighted columns of Peace's main building. This time I felt I was looking at a night-lit Tara. I came to town another time or few before arriving to stay, once to the Angus Barn restaurant, once to a party at the apartment of an N.C. State student, where I glimpsed a boy I'd known in high school looking entirely grown-up and heading happily to a back room with two chilled glasses of white wine. Raleigh had started to feel faintly thrilling in an older-than-school-days way.

Indeed it was romance of my own that would keep me in the Triangle area after graduation in 1970, and that lingering would outlast the romance and ultimately make me a Raleighite. But first an ordeal: Senior year I spent six weeks as a practice teacher so that my English major would give me an income in case being-a-writer didn't work out.

Never has a student teacher been luckier in her assignment, or more miserable. I was sent to teach "accelerated" classes at Raleigh's Needham Broughton High School under the supervision of beloved teacher Lou Rosser. An ideal situation. But I didn't want to teach; didn't want to be an enforcer of rules trapped in a classroom trying unsuccessfully to engage groups of thirty, many of whom, like me, would rather have been elsewhere. Apparently that attitude showed. One afternoon I was sitting at my desk in a corner of the room, recovering from the day. A student appeared—Ira, a wild-haired boy carrying, unbelievably, a briefcase. "Miss Payne," he said, "we're going to get through this." Unforgettable words. The next day he began to present in class a thoroughly worked-out alternative to my interpretation of *Moby Dick,* which we'd just "taken up." About half the class supported his argument and the others took my side. A fiercely competitive debate raged day after day. Ira was right: We got through it.

The Broughton dogwood tree also helped me during those godawful weeks. In the school's courtyard was the largest bearer of the state flower that I had ever seen: three stories, magnificent, and in bloom during my tenure. Less pleasing: The principal, Dr. Jewell, volunteered that my skirts were too short. And I had a run-in with the widely admired English teacher, Phyllis Peacock, whose former students included novelists Anne Tyler and Reynolds Price. If she encouraged me to become a writer it was only indirectly. Our classes were meeting together one day to listen to student oral reports. I welcomed this as a wonderful opportunity to zone out and take a rest, until Mrs. Peacock called on me to discuss one of the student reports. I did not come to share the popular enthusiasm for her teaching methods.

I was, instead, about to become a Raleigh newspaper reporter, much more to my liking. Mid-spring, I put on what I viewed as a grown-up ensemble (which the editor would later tell me was the shortest skirt he'd ever seen; no school rules for me!) and went to the *News & Observer* building on McDowell Street. In the elevator, I asked the nearest person where to apply for a job. "Second floor," he said. So that's where I went. Turns out the second floor was not the home of the morning paper I was familiar with, but instead housed the afternoon paper, the *Raleigh Times,* which I had never heard of. I had the job by the time I'd understood what I'd applied for—perhaps not the best sign of my skill as an investigative reporter.

And so I moved to Raleigh to live and work full-time, an adult and a proud new Raleighite, in spite of the itchy awkwardness of my previous six weeks here. Like my Aunt Betty I was a "single girl in the city," though

I was arriving about the same time as the women's movement and soon would drop the titles of *Miss* and *girl*. My first address here was a big, wide-porched tourist home on Hillsborough Street. In the mornings before work, I'd walk to Baxley's diner—I didn't know then that it was a Raleigh institution—and sit at the counter, swigging a tall orange juice to prepare for the day. *The Raleigh Times* turned out to be the better place for me to work. The staff was a small feisty band of friends, gleefully competitive with the *N&O*, with terrific *esprit de corps*. Our newsroom was the throbbing center of the world.

I was assigned the health/medicine/science beat, which included the new environmental movement. I wrote about hospital politics and clinic expansions and about how polluted the proposed Jordan Lake southwest of the city was likely to be. Eventually, I moved to an apartment at one of the city's few complexes, located off Avent Ferry Road. Driving to work, I often played the raucous rock musical *Tommy* to wake myself up; and I'd feel triumphant as I came over a green hill on Western Boulevard and saw the sun coming up in a ruddy haze behind the medieval fortress of Central Prison.

One midmorning I set off to cover the governor's press conference—quite a heady assignment only weeks into my new adult life. I found myself walking the few blocks to Governor Bob Scott's office accompanied by *N&O* editor Claude Sitton and *Raleigh Times* editor Herb O'Keefe. Towering in heels between them, I felt like a gangly and intimidated young giraffe. Claude said he'd heard there was a room in one of the nearby old houses that was filled with nothing but stacks of *News & Observers*. "Oh, I have a room like that," I glibly offered and got a laugh. Happily running for Queen of the World, I felt genuinely sorry for my friends who didn't work for the *Raleigh Times*.

But the truth was my rooms were full of novels, not news. I'd never paid any attention to government before starting the job; having been fortunate in life, I'd blindly assumed everything was working alright. Thus, politically you could have called me conservative, ignorant, pig-headed, or all of these. Raleigh and reporting and hanging out with reporters quickly changed that.

Education was added to my beat just in time for desegregation of the local schools in 1971 (Broughton had been a white high school when I taught there a year earlier). I was no more prepared to read a Supreme Court ruling and write an interpretation of the effect on Raleigh (in under two hours!) than I was to be an astronaut. But I covered the nights of public hearings, the uproar—directed one evening at me personally— and the relatively smooth process of integration here. At the same time, I broadened my own outlook—even my eyes actually looked older when it was over. What I'd thought was a temporary sign of fatigue was the first hint of crow's feet. I decided, once the big story was over, to get out of hard news where I didn't really belong.

So I quit my job and became a freelancer, which might seem a bold move but really wasn't since I came from a family of the self-employed. The day I gave notice I got home to my apartment and found in the mail that I'd sold my first magazine piece: a rewrite of a story I'd done for the paper about Saint Augustine's College's mobile recruiting office. *College Management* was prepared to pay me $35: dreadful, but almost half my rent at the time. It was a fairly realistic introduction to freelancing.

My new career was exciting, but working out of my bedroom was dismal. I'd often find pages of notes in my unmade bed. Once to escape the quiet, I went out to lunch, by myself, to Darryl's, its booths decorated in what seemed to be variations of a frontier theme. I was escorted to a table located, of all places, inside a jail cell. Looking out through those bars, I knew I was going to have to make a change.

So I rented a tiny office ($36 a month) downtown on the seventh floor of the Odd Fellows Building, subletting half to another writer to help with the rent and keep me company. The space was just wider than the two windows that provided us a gorgeous view of sunset every day over Raleigh's western treeline.

During the Seventies, I married, lived at the then-wooded north edge of the city, then unmarried and moved back inside the Beltline, to share with two women one of those old townhouses in Raleigh's liberal heart: Cameron Park. I'd begun doing a lot of travel writing, and my new location was only steps from the airport shuttle at the Brownstone Hotel, long a temporary home for many a state legislator. I'd also gotten religion and become a devoted member of the activist Pullen Memorial Baptist Church, only half a block from my doorstep.

And I was single again in the city. As one might refer to a pod of whales, a covey of quail, a stand of trees, what I had then for nine complex years was a turbulence of gentleman callers. Where there is government, there are men; my initial romantic vibes about the place were right.

Twice between romances, I considered leaving and moving to New York, a place that glows for me like Duke Chapel. I'd never meant to stay in this small-ish, not-exotic, nothing-too-fancy city. But my roots here had grown too deep, and New York was expensive, and travel writing could always take me out on the road. Besides, I didn't want to lose the damp crickets-and-frogs feel of a Southern summer night. The moment I made my decision for the second and final time, I was out for a late evening run, just back from a few days in midtown Manhattan. A street-light shone white against the dew on the massive shrubs along the edge of the road. Hardly any sound other than my footfalls. But it was the feel of the air that decided me; the warm humid weight of it felt fertile, rich. I thought to myself: Guess I'm staying.

At the same time, a change I was certain I'd made had come undone. I found I hadn't left hard news behind at all. As a freelancer, I'd become the Norfolk paper's part-time woman-in-Raleigh writing two stories a week about actions affecting the northeastern North Carolina counties. The first time I stepped inside the House chamber of the N.C. General Assembly, I felt as if I were looking at a huge popcorn popper on hot boil with no lid and was in fact standing in that hot pan of oil. Legislators were jumping up and sitting down again, crouching to confer with each other, rushing in and out of the chamber while others were speaking. I saw no pattern or purpose. After meeting that day's deadline, I would have plenty more time to learn. For eleven years I wrote about North Carolina state government for the *Virginian-Pilot;* for three of those years I added a gig as a three-night-a-week talking head on UNC-TV's live legislative news program.

About Jones Street, as some refer to the general assembly: It is, of course, where Daddy came to get money for the college. It's where a lot of people come to try to get money, and it is a mad scrambling world unto itself. I always felt that I entered the building in January and emerged in summer, having missed spring altogether. Rushing through the labyrinth of halls, I resolved one season that, on finding my target, I would say hello before asking my questions. That didn't last long. When I finally quit hard news once again, I came away with two enduring beliefs: One, it takes courage to run for public office; and, two, that *Robert's Rules of Order* must be stronger than the law of gravity to have successfully prevented bloodshed in that building for so long. Those rooms are a setting for passion, conflict, high drama, triumph, brutal disappointment—and long tedious meetings. And romance. Example: one of my brothers (Harry) was a legislator from New Hanover for six terms and married *N&O* reporter/columnist Ruth Sheehan.

I fell in love and got married again myself, to Raleigh psychologist Bob Dick. We met, not in the legislature, but at a book launch party a few blocks away for Angela Davis-Gardner's first novel. By that time I had begun writing fiction and, to better support that habit, begun writing ad and brochure copy for local businesses and agencies. Of course Raleigh would show up in my fiction; my third novel, *Cobalt Blue*, has some crucial tense moments in a senator's office, and my first one, *Revelation*, takes place in a church a lot like Raleigh's Pullen.

My marriage threw a major twist into my relationship with the city. I moved in with Bob, forty minutes from town in a log house in the woods of adjoining Chatham County. In short, I became a commuter, because Raleigh wouldn't let me go. Most days I come into town to write and to work with other writers, leaving behind a stereotypically writerly setting, quiet, solitude, etc. I love our rural home, my garden, and kayaking at nearby gorgeous Jordan Lake, which indeed has had predicted pollution problems I long ago wrote about. But to get work done I need to put on my go-to-town clothes and take the long ride back to the place where there's traffic, noise, gossip, news, people to eat lunch with.

My office is now at the downtown edge of the Victorian-era neighborhood of Oakwood where I share space with writer-friend Carrie Knowles in her building, which she has named Free Range Studio. The place is only a couple of blocks from the house I first visited here so many years ago. I often eat lunch at the K&W Cafeteria in Cameron Village (the one that was in Belk's downtown on my first visit is long gone). Restaurants are a sign of how much more cosmopolitan the city has become these recent decades. It was a slow process. The exotic restaurants when I first arrived were the Canton Cafe, Amedeo's, and the International House of Pancakes. I had dined in New Delhi as a travel writer long before there was an Indian restaurant here. Now there's Indian, Thai, Vietnamese, a long list of Japanese, and more.

For a while I was part of a group of novelists who met for lunch at the Brownstone.

One day someone brought a guest, a French woman, a Raleighite originally from Paris. One of our number inquired how she happened to move to Raleigh. "Romance," was her one-word answer, though she pronounced it *rrrohhmanhhs*. In France, she had met a man from here . . . and so on. With a straight face, her questioner said, "I guess a lot of people move from Paris to Raleigh for romance." We laughed, because Raleigh is a regular normal small city: no distinguishing features like the Eiffel Tower or the Seine, no ocean, no Alps, no beaches or central river as in my hometown.

And yet: I remember my first visit as a five-year-old, excited and bedazzled by the traffic of Fayetteville Street. Nearly sixty years later, I still am roused by the city view as I ride into town on South Saunders Street. It's a complicated relationship, of course, this business of Raleigh and me; because the place isn't New York and it isn't Paris and I didn't set out to stay here. But looking back now, I think I rightly can call it a romance. In fact, I'm sure I can.

PEGGY PAYNE is the author of novels *Revelation, Sister India,* and *Cobalt Blue.* Her travel writing has taken her to more than twenty-five countries; her work has appeared in many major newspapers and magazines, including *More, Cosmopolitan, Family Circle, Ms.,* and *Travel & Leisure.* www.peggypayne.com.

Patterns

TRACIE FELLERS

DECEMBER 1997

"Why?"

That's what my mother says when I tell her, while we were finishing our Sunday dinner—post-Thanksgiving plates of turkey, oyster dressing, collard greens, and sweet potatoes, all of which we cooked ourselves, plus mashed potatoes, gravy, and cranberry relish, courtesy of Boston Market. Mom and I had joked as we finished our cooking on Thanksgiving afternoon, speculating that my maternal grandmother and my mother's only sister, the two great cooks in our family, were peering down from their heavenly seats, chuckling over my mother Phyllis and that baby Tracie in the kitchen. I could just imagine Grandma and Aunt Bunny sitting together in some celestial place, their eyes full of laughter, leaning close together to nudge each other over the two of us chopping and mixing and measuring.

I tell Mom, from my seat next to hers at the kitchen table, that I have something to do upstairs before I head back to my apartment on Hillsborough Street, in walking distance of N.C. State, this afternoon. My plan is to go up to her bedroom, to her walk-in closet. To take a look at my debutante ball dress, the taffeta gown that has sat undisturbed since she sent it to the cleaners to be boxed up and "preserved" for posterity some fourteen years ago. I'm not sure exactly when she ferried the dress over to one of Durham's oldest dry cleaners. But I do know it couldn't have been long after the Alpha Kappa Alpha Debutante Ball in late November 1983, which linked me with ninety-eight other young African American women in a Raleigh coming-of-age ritual, one dating back almost half a century.

The ball, as tradition dictated, was on the Friday following Thanksgiving—just eleven days after my Aunt Bunny, the hands and mind and spirit behind my debutante dress, died in a freak car accident.

"You have the pictures," my mother says, clearly trying to discourage this peculiar idea of mine, this notion I have of dragging the oversized box containing the dress out of her closet, tearing the tape away from the cardboard, feeling the weight of the heavy fabric in my hands, perhaps even draping the dress on my frame once again. Pictures alone won't do, I try to explain to her.

But what I don't say is that after close to fifteen years, I need to make the dress—the most tangible symbol I have of my aunt's love for me—real again. My mother is right. I have a stack of pictures and my memory as proof that the dress existed. That my aunt, Bernice Morgan, had sewn it, ruffles, carefully chosen beads, translucent sequins, and all. I know that I once swirled around a ballroom floor in it. But I need to know that the dress, a singularly powerful manifestation of my Aunt Bunny's legacy, exists still. I don't want to rely on what I remember.

Michael Reynolds, author of an acclaimed five-volume biography of Ernest Hemingway, writes eloquently about the fallibility of memory. In his essay on the limits of biography, Reynolds is both incisive and graceful in his prose, describing the past as "malleable, various, and continually changing, a place of dreams." Lately, his words ring especially true—even painfully so—as I search my own memory, summoning up what I recall of wearing the dress, of those moments shadowed by my aunt's death.

Even the most unanalytical and unconcerned observer could not help but associate the creator, my aunt, with her creation, the dress. But the link between the dress and Aunt Bunny's death resonates far beyond the obvious, beyond what one can clearly see on the surface. Making the dress for the debutante ball, a formal celebration of my arrival at the threshold of womanhood, was one of my aunt's last creative acts, and hers was a life inscribed and illuminated by her great capacity for creativity.

Bernice Morgan brought her innovative mind to bear in the classroom, where she developed strategies to reach out to children with behavioral and developmental problems. And she was just as inventive in the many homes she had during her life, a life in which she, my uncle, and twin cousins moved from New York to North Carolina, then later to Delaware, Maryland, and ultimately Philadelphia. Aunt Bunny sewed everything from clothes to curtains, decorated with as much flair as any professional interior designer, and painted everything from cityscapes, which she framed and hung on her living room walls, to a backyard hopscotch grid that I remember fondly from her house in Durham in the 1970s.

She also found joy and took pride in her mastery in the kitchen, where she kept a pot of Chock full o'Nuts coffee going—her java of choice since her days in New York. And if you were lucky, she'd slice you a generous piece of her unbelievably rich carrot cake to go with it. But I don't think even I have been willing to see how much the presence of the one— the debutante dress, inanimate, mute, and shut away in a box—marks the absence of the other, my aunt, whose boundless energy, big heart, restless spirit, gift of gab and gracious hostessing, and love of fun and family were too quickly and shockingly taken.

Maybe that's why I'm so bent on freeing the dress from its cocoon of paper and preservatives, at least for a short while. My mother observes me from the bathroom door, her eyes intent and watchful behind her glasses, as I pry open the cardboard covering to reach a smaller box within. The box is white, with a blue plastic window and a brownish bow design. Pretty tacky, I can't help thinking. I remember my debutante dress of moire taffeta, a fabric with the appearance of watered silk, as opulent- and elegant-looking. It had taken my aunt days, maybe weeks of searching Philadelphia's version of a garment district—nothing like what she'd been accustomed to in New York—to find the fabric.

As much as I want to make the dress a material presence once more, not just something that exists in my memory, and as much as I want to hold it to me, to take in the fine gloss of the fabric, to admire my aunt's craftsmanship and care, it is what the dress has come to represent—the love and kinship of spirit that flowed between my aunt and me—that brought me back to it. And it's that thought, my image of the dress as vessel, that nags me most as I look at the packaging. That dress, my dress, *our* dress deserves better safekeeping than the home it found in that cheesy box.

My dismay deepens when I finally open the box enough to extract the gown that my aunt had spent months shaping and sewing without the benefit of a pattern. I had envisioned a carefully pressed and folded dress, perhaps enveloped in folds of tissue paper. But there's no tissue, and there are no careful folds of taffeta as I unceremoniously pull a crumpled gown from the half-opened box. No matter, I tell myself, though the lack of more thoughtful care for my dress, an irreplaceable piece of my history, makes me angry for a moment. What really matters is that I'm holding it in my hands.

For the first time since I was sixteen years old, I touch my aunt's handiwork. I spread the dress out on my mother's bed and run my hand across its skirt; it feels substantial and silken under my fingers. I examine the ruffled neckline, not too high, not too low, and find tiny pearl-like beads there. I had forgotten those, as surely as I had forgotten that the location for the ball was the Raleigh Civic Center, not Memorial Auditorium. I notice that the sleeve edges, and the five ruffles that ripple down the skirt, from front to back, are subtly accented with translucent sequins, unobtrusive enough to go unnoticed in daylight, but perhaps present enough to lend sparkle to the dress on the night of the ball. I see that the hem of the dress is yellowing and wonder why, and what I can do to stop it. But the only thing I can do, I decide, is to try the dress on.

I often find it hard to believe, but I'm thirty now, soon to be thirty-one. I once thought I might get married in my debutante dress. But I've come to realize that more likely than not, I'll never wear it again.

So I tie on the hoop slip that was bought for me to wear underneath the dress fourteen years ago. I've never been large, but my adult frame—partly because of two years of what I jokingly call the grad school diet—lacks some of the girlish roundness of my adolescent figure. As a result, the hoop slip, which makes me feel like some postmodern parody of Scarlett in *Gone with the Wind*, hangs off my waist, and it takes me a while to adjust it enough to slip into my dress.

With the dress on, I carefully step into my mother's bathroom first. But the mirror there only allows me to see the dress from neckline to just below the waist. So I rustle down the stairs, feeling more like Scarlett than ever—until I reach the closest thing to a full-length mirror in my mom's townhouse, in the downstairs bathroom. Looking in that mirror, I see the dress still molds itself to my frame. Closer to ivory than pure white in the light of the bathroom, it had, in every sense of the word, been made for me. But when I last wore it as a sixteen-year-old high school senior in 1983, I was a girl. Moving toward womanhood, yes, but still very much a girl.

In photos taken the night of the debutante ball, at the old Radisson in downtown Raleigh, I can see the glow, the hope and promise in the eyes of that girl in the one-of-a-kind dress. I remember laughing with my cousins as we walked down Fayetteville Street later that night, not venturing far from the hotel, a brisk fall wind blowing at our backs. I have no memory of where we were going, but I do recall still being caught up in the emotions of the evening. Missing my aunt, but enjoying the feeling that the night was mine, a harbinger of the life I had ahead of me.

I had been alert, aware, attuned to the world around me, I like to think. Yet I was unworldly, too. Unknowing about so much that life would bring.

My face hasn't changed much. But the image facing me in the mirror this Sunday afternoon is that of a woman. I can see traces of loss, like the loss of my aunt, who isn't here to see my attempts to use all the pieces of the pattern she left me. But the set of my shoulders and the lift of my head also have been marked by the triumphs that have come along the way. Like Aunt Bunny—teacher, seamstress, cook extraordinaire, artist, mother, sister, daughter, friend—I'm making it up as I go.

TRACIE FELLERS is a writer and editor whose Raleigh roots come from her father's side of the family tree. She started her career writing for daily newspapers in North Carolina and Virginia, and her fiction has appeared in *Long Story Short, Obsidian,* and *roger.* Her creative nonfiction has been published in the journal *Sing Heavenly Muse!* A graduate of Northwestern University, North Carolina State University, and the University of North Carolina at Greensboro, she has received awards for her fiction from North Carolina State University and the National Council for Black Studies.

Intersections

JUNE SPENCE

SINCE 2003, I'VE LIVED with my husband and, more recently, our sons, in the Five Points neighborhood of Georgetown. I'm a third-generation resident of Five Points, though by chance, not design. My husband moved to Raleigh from Philadelphia in 1992, and soon afterward he chose the late 1930s-era stucco house for its closeness to downtown, its charm, and its cheapness, not necessarily in that order.

Once my husband and I had cast our lots together, embracing the house's myriad fissures and slopes, and even its position on the gamier end of Five Points, settling here for the long haul felt a bit like fate. These days most of the area is considered quite desirable, with the inflated home values to back it up, though along our sketchier stretch there are still a few troubled souls afoot and dubious curbside transactions conducted, not always under cover of darkness. The split-levels and strip malls of my north Raleigh upbringing can't compare with the randomly gentrifying rows of bungalows and shotguns along the Norfolk Southern railroad line, where my father's ghost and mine trundle back and forth, sometimes lurching alongside each other, sometimes diverging.

It's a short walk to my grandparents' old house on Mial Street in the Hi-Mount district, a house I stayed at for days and sometimes weeks at a time as a child, eating peanut butter candy and watching TV with lawless abandon. When I'd had my fill of sugar and *The Partridge Family*, I would rearrange the curio shelves, try on dusky blond wigs, and sort buttons, cloth remnants, and scratched stacks of 78s. I would search sepia-toned photographs for my grandfather's handsome scowl, which I recognized even in his baby picture, and my grandmother's beautifully marcelled hair and home-sewn dresses. I alternated between staying up late with my grandmother and waking up early with my grandfather, who kept a milk-man's hours long into retirement.

When my father was a boy, they lived in a Hi-Mount duplex, renting out the other half. In his teens, they lived on Glenwood Avenue, just south of the complex Five Points intersection, where no amount of signage seems to clarify right-of-way. Facing the Rialto Theatre (formerly the Colony) is the large, stately house, now an attorney's office, they rented for a spell so there'd be enough room for my uncle's wife and four young children to live with them.

My grandmother referred to the four as "my other children," when she spoke of them, which wasn't often. I didn't understand who she meant at the time. They were gone, taken to Indiana by their mother, long before my days of peanut butter candy-binging and button-sorting on Mial Street.

In my father's day, Georgetown and Hi-Mount were working-class neighborhoods, Hayes Barton's poor relations, where the races lived together but didn't mingle; vacant lots and the scrubby areas surrounding the county rest home provided neutral zones for white and black kids to play. The meandering route my father took through town as a boy was full of such interstitial spaces. He brought a black friend home once and wasn't whipped for it like he'd been the time he drank from the "colored" fountain at the bus station. But he understood just as clearly that this was not to be repeated.

He didn't think his parents were right, but then, almost nothing that grown-ups insisted on made any sense. Why, for example, had they sent him away to live with his grandmother in Angier until she was the only one he knew as Mama, only to wrench him away from her and bring him back to Raleigh a year later? He hadn't been old enough to comprehend what tuberculosis meant, or how lucky his mother had been to survive it before antibiotics, when they could offer only isolation, rest, and regular injections of gas into the chest to surround and collapse the diseased lung.

My father roamed Five Points throughout the Forties and Fifties with his older brother and a group of boys who called themselves the Northside Gang, when it was still Raleigh's north side. Boys as young as five and six tagged along with the older boys to throw rocks, smoke cigarettes, explore the storm-water tunnels, and smash the bottles of grape pop that remained in heaps by an abandoned plant, after first prying off the caps and drinking the contents. My father still carries the scar of the skin graft he got after flinging a broken bottle; as the jagged glass left his grip it took the tip of his finger with it.

He and his friends shot steel-tipped arrows straight up into the sky and dared each other not to look as they came back down. The boy who did look up was scorned as a chicken, though he lost an eye. A favored prank was to surprise drivers on Whitaker Mill Road by placing a cardboard box in the street with the smallest boy concealed inside. They accidentally set ablaze a grove of trees with an oil filter they'd scavenged and lit, intending only to heat their fort.

They were all reckless bordering on calamitous, but my father would get to wondering when God might hold him accountable, and that stayed his hand when the others stole from the neighborhood grocery or worse. My uncle knew no such limits; he was among the older kids who cranked up all the school buses in the dead of night and let them bash into each other. Later he stole cars and drank his way out of the navy.

"You're going to wind up in the penitentiary," my grandfather warned him often. That made it no less shocking when as a young man, and already a father, my uncle teamed up with an older, more violent sociopath for a liquor-and-pill-fueled spree that began with a voluntary admission into Dorothea Dix asylum—then a common means for drunks to avoid jail—and ended in Greensboro and the deaths of three people they'd encountered along the way.

His wife fled with their children to spare them the aftermath, understandably, though the grief of losing them too lay heavy over my grandparents. It's a wonder they could bear to stay in the neighborhood— everyone would have known what their son did—but the proximity of friends must have brought comfort. My grandfather wasn't a churchgoer, but my grandmother could walk to Emmanuel Baptist, where she sang in the choir. Perhaps they'd been reluctant to stray too far in case their "other children" came back. (They did, as adults.)

My uncle's crimes are the family narrative that cast a pall over all the others; they trivialized my father's own struggles and diminished too many of his successes. Still, the most astonishing story is the one that happened in its shadow: the happy childhood my parents and grandparents conspired to give me and my sister, and which they largely delivered—much of it within these few short blocks.

When I walk on Whitaker Mill Road, the artery dividing my past and present life, I pass the same bungalows I passed hand in hand with my grandmother on the long trek to the Pine State Creamery on Glenwood Avenue, where my grandfather worked and would give us ice cream in a fluted cup to eat with a small wooden paddle. I also cross the meandering paths my father took, with his gang or unaccompanied, required only to stay within earshot of his father's summoning whistle that meant get home in five minutes or bring a switch. I pass the sanitarium that confined his mother, now a nursing home where my other grandmother spent her final days. I walk the same block where my father once spotted Five Points' first television antenna rising from a rooftop and broke into a run when he realized it was his.

Meantime, my sons amble up these same sidewalks, moving through our vapor pasts.

JUNE SPENCE is the author of *Missing Women and Others*, a collection of short stories, and *Change Baby*, a novel. She has taught creative writing at University of North Carolina at Chapel Hill, Vanderbilt University, Meredith College, North Carolina State University, Berry College, and Bowling Green State University. She freelances in corporate communications and blogs in fits and starts at unshelvedblog.wordpress.com.

Fair Ground

TOM HAWKINS

I courted my wives at the State Fair—
my late wife Anna
and my living wife Sylvia—
lode stars, novas, cosmic
transformations.
This was not my method,
courting at the State Fair,
where for me romance
just happened twice
in that big breathing
harvest festival ritual event
rising from the land.

The Fairgrounds stand at what was once
the edge of town, 344 acres, just about
the size of two North Carolina family farms.
All year the Fairgrounds gestate and percolate
with shows for dogs, horses, cats,
gems crystals and beads, the circus,
home decor, Christmas crafts,
classic automobile auctions, hot rods,
boats, fishing, recreational vehicles,
tobacco pipes, coins and stamps, guns.
And the weekend flea market.

The Fairgrounds sit at the intersection
of Blue Ridge Road, home of the
State Police and the Museum of Art,
and Hillsborough Street that stretches
from the State Capitol downtown to
the small town of Hillsborough—by way of

roads with other names — site of early
dissent that led to the Revolutionary War.
The Fairgrounds border the Southern Railroad tracks
where the trains roar and wail.
The fair's landmarks are the Spanish castles of
the Education and Commercial Buildings
with their fluttering flags and pendants,
and the sway-backed roof of Dorton Arena,
a modern architectural sight but vast and barren
inside, where musicians making comebacks
shout out their well-worn tunes.

Two weeks before the fair all commerce halts.
Trucks bearing the steel frames of rides
and a sprawling town of rolling homes arrive.
A construction site sets up and lines form
at the hiring hall. The carny folk build
and elevator inspectors check out the bolted steel.
Thirty-seven years I've watched the fair foal,
evaded the traffic that it brought,
fought my way to parking
and walked in from afar
or took a bus to its
numbered entry gates, run-down discount tickets;
now that I am sixty-five, they let me in free.

The first fairs I knew, I staffed a booth
on veterans' benefits and came to know the fair
at lunch or after work. For lunch it was the
now long gone Raleigh Women's Club cafeteria,
a meat and two vegetables, ice tea and pie,

for about three dollars forty-five cents.
From those days I remember the chant:
"Little people, little people. Look down at your feet,
look up at your knees. That's how tall they are!"
That went along with the world's biggest horse,
the world's largest alligator.

Barkers chant above the drumming of generators
for the rides, the shrieks of people in the churning cages
and plummeting parachute drops, the centrifugal
cylinders slowly losing their floors and the pirate ships
with rows of citizens weightless in their seats.
The whole cacophony a chord of sheet metal torn
across a treble cleft of screams.
"Guess your weight or guess your age. Win a prize.
Every child wins. Step right over here."

The soul of the fair is an animal soul,
dwarf rabbits, huge floppy-eared white ones,
chickens — Wyandottes, Javas, Lemonas, Chanteclers —
look you in the eyes.
Young people leading their young animals
on tethers, girls and boys with vivid faces
full of caution and longing,
as their calves, goats, ewes and rams step
reluctantly, delicately after them,
out of the garden of fields and ponds
into the tall pens and looming grandstands,
tugging at their halters in youth and expectation.

The year of the tigers, Anna's last fair, the handlers
brought their toothy cats, each spotted with
white dots behind the ears, sinewy appetites contained
in a loose maze of rolling connected cages.
The broad striped faces sized up children from their bars
like diners studying entrees in a cafeteria line
before the keepers fed them slabs of horse
they offered at the ends of long stout rusty forks.
Our eyes devoured their slinking energy,
supplied the wilds their mythic muscles longed to hunt.
Anna wove ahead into the crowd, suddenly lost
into the tiger night sky.

One widower year I wandered the garden exhibit and produce
sipping at a Mountain Laurel tobacco pipe by a craftsman carver
who sells at the fair, smoke evoking absence.
Every year by decades the hall of decorated cakes,
canned goods, selected-for-perfection fruit,
visionary quilts, hand-sewn children's clothes and gowns,
the quiet nightly labors of hands and minds
inching through the incandescent light and night noises
to public view, patience and passion distilled.

I always go to the hot cider stand
especially if the day or night is cold.

The air resounds.
I have worked, I have worked;
I have done the work of the world six days
and this is my seventh of rest,
the work of the world,

the perfect evening dress
that holds its hanger with
exquisite stitching,
the cherry pie someone has wrested
from the sweet trees' fruit,
plucked from reach
of birds' beaks,
bread folded in the respirating yeast
of the dough, and charmed
in the heat of the oven's alcove
until its fragrant chords resound
through all the pipes and stops.

Or this calf I have heaved
from its mother's belly
in the dark before dawn
and tugged to its feet,
have picked up with its legs
shimmed against my arms
its fifty pounds
and fed lespedeza and sweet hay,
and I have brought my calf here
to the crowd of human view,
to the consideration of puzzling minds,
to the competition,
the champion and reserve,
the doomed champions,
the human spheres,
the rules of which are listed
in two hundred-some pages
of categories and criteria

from zinnias to yearling goats,
from Charolais, Angus, Guernsey,
to mock pound cake.

And when you're hungry,
the food stands in their trailers
with seating under tents
can fry nearly any food —
mushrooms, candy bars,
ice cream, donuts,
funnel cakes, Italian sausage,
cheeseburgers, turkey legs.

When your legs tire out
after nine o'clock at night,
the pyrotechnic crew does the fireworks
over the field under the grandstand.
Di-boom, dittily-boom.
We get away from recorded music to hear
the musical drumbeat in the light.

(The Latin word "feria"
means holy day. In Medieval England
the fair was franchised by the crown
or parliament. In Scotland, "the Holy Fair"
meant a sacramental occasion.)

My first state fair, after a long day
at the Veterans' table, many faces
and too much friendly explaining,
I phoned Anna at her sublet townhouse

a crow's mile away, and invited her
to the fair one night I had off,
with the evening finale of fireworks
popping behind me in the cool fall air,
so she could hear them in stereo,
both across town and over the phone,
where I heard her symphonic voice
accept, where the household cats
tensed their ears at popping bombs.

Thirty years later, ten years after Anna
transcended with her voice,
Sylvia and I entered that same
lavish Fairgrounds that roared distantly
as we approached erupting with
the energy the red clay fields set forth
at harvest. The minds of animals
tunneled through the human event
staking the sky to the soil
and surrounding human wishes.
As an only child farm girl,
Sylvia raised a calf,
hefted it between her arms,
baked the prize-winning cake,
stitched garments to be judged.

So we are here over years millions strong,
through the numbered gates,
the midway, the bingo,
the gardens, the animal barns,
where encampments of farm kids

will sleep listening to their cattle
breathe and the multi-various
chickens cluck and crow
their wire-cage declamations,
pied beauty of their short-lived
angelic plumed selves.
I embrace the smallness of self
that helps me understand
my particle of the universe.

On this red clay earth, hard packed
or below the grandstand plowed up
to make a stage for tractor and horse,
the white-Stetsoned ghost of
Jim Graham, the late Agricultural
Commissioner and farmers' friend,
when tobacco reigned a fading king,
the ghosts of Anna's and my youth
roaming the exhibits whole days,
amidst the rides and games

Sylvia and I line up for State University
ice cream, cider, a gospel choir.
Sylvia knows all the hymns' words.
In a pen, a camel works its prehensile lips
and discerns the character of men.
The mighty Percheron mare
shields her gangly colt from the passing faces.
Here I am again, one age at a time,
another year, another three hundred pound
pumpkin, another vat of pickles to be guessed.

The fair has slowly migrated
to the Fairgrounds of my brain.
Holidays, holy days, ten days in October,
the crisping of the years.
Through high wide sunshine,
clouds one year, another rain,
the feet tramping on their pilgrimage,
a day off and a day, the grandparents,
the kids, the scrambling parents,
the couples holding hands.

I won't go this year. It's too expensive.
We can't get the wheelchair across the
rutted muddy parking lot, and
how far do you think you can walk?
It always comes around, the fall,
the shortening days, the awakening
of night, the distant howls and
yammering of the crowd
like the churning of the sea.
I remember this.
It could have been another life.
It might have been, was, and is.
I've been here before.

TOM HAWKINS has lived in Raleigh since 1975. He poetry has been published in literary magazines since the 1960s. He has a book of short and short-short stories, *Paper Crown*, from BkMk Press at University of Missouri-Kansas City. His literary work has appeared in several editions of *The Norton Anthology of American Literature*.

Home is where you mend the roof

JULIANA MAKUCHI NFAH-ABBENYI

SUNDAY. 2AM.

I'm jolted out of sleep. I do not recognize the number. "Hello." Silence. I hang up.

My home phone rings again. I say, "Hello." Twice. I hang up again. Who's calling me from Africa? I know it's not a Cameroon number. The 242 country code looks familiar but the number my caller id displays isn't my brother's. My iPhone interrupts my thoughts. "Hello." The connection holds. Still no answer on the other end. I hang up. My son opens my bedroom door. Who is it? he asks, standing in the doorway. He has that look on his face. Many an African immigrant to the United States would recognize that look. That dreaded 2am-phone-call-look; the albatross around our necks. I don't know. I don't recognize the number, I say. Why don't you call them back? he says. I shrug slowly pulling the sheets up to my shoulders. Whoever it is will call back, I say. Are you sure? Maybe you should call them, Maku. Aah, it's okay, I say. Okay. Goodnight, Maku. He gives me one last glance and gently shuts the door. Someone's about to ruin my spring break, I mumble, pulling the sheets over my head.

I want to go back to sleep. Five minutes later, I stick my hand out; grab the home phone and hit redial. "We're sorry your call cannot be completed as dialed." I swear at Time Warner Cable as I slam the phone down on the nightstand. I grab my cell phone and hit redial. "Hello." My brother's voice; crystal clear. Relief.

"My brother! How are you?"

"I'm fine."

"Are you back from South Africa?"

"Yes."

"How was the trip? How was Cape Town?"

"Everything went well."

"Good."

"I just have to work on my report . . . but I'm calling because I have bad news . . ."

"Someone's dead."

"Yes."

"Who?"

"Fr. Sylvester."

"When?"

"This morning. I just got off the phone with Timothy. Timothy called me yesterday. Not long after I got back. He told me Fr. Sylvester was sick. I called and talked to Fr. Sylvester for twenty minutes . . ."

My forty-one-year-old brother, Rev. Sylvester Nsemelah Nfah, died in his bed, sometime before dawn on Sunday 03/03/13 in Bamenda, in the North West Region of Cameroon. In the winter, Cameroon is six hours ahead of Eastern Standard Time. Daylight Saving Time arrives exactly in one week. That 2am call brought anguish to my bed in Raleigh, N.C., as people in Bamenda were rising to a new dawn and getting ready for mass. News of the death of a loved one unsettles even the most laid-back immigrant once it reaches its destination somewhere in America. It is the one thing that has the power to disrupt the structured sense of place that African immigrants cultivate whether as permanent resident aliens or as naturalized citizens. When one is thousands of miles away from what used to be home, one expects, one day or another, to hear about a sudden death for it is said that no one in Africa dies of natural causes. This is of course the psychological mask one dons in the pretense that a loss in the family is one more occasion for celebrating life, no matter. I wear this shield in the hope it would protect me from the heartache; from that invisible accusing finger that blames faraway calamities at home to my abandonment; to my quest for personal fulfillment. One brother dies, then a second, then a third, and now a fourth brother joins the group of siblings departed. And my shield endures yet another crack. It is as if I have to begin all over again. I moved to Raleigh, N.C., in June 2006. I have slowly, in the last seven years, been making Raleigh home. I was even becoming blasé about the success of this project. And all it takes is a phone call, this one in the dead of night while I am ensconced in the warmth of my comfortable bed, to shatter any illusion of that neat separation between home there and home here. Feelings not of loss but of helplessness abound. You wish you were a character on *Star Trek*. You yearn to say "Beam me up, Scotty!"and in the blink of an eye, I'm right there in Bamenda, standing side by side my dad and siblings, crying in each other's arms, dashing from neighborhood to neighborhood making preparations, having heated arguments—sometimes calmly, sometimes screaming, sometimes laughing—over who has done what and who was supposed to do what and who hasn't done what and who needs to do what. Twenty-first-century Globalization lulls us into believing that one can simply reach out and touch someone else; someone in America can reach out and touch someone in Bangladesh; someone in China can reach out and touch someone in Cape Verde, so the experts quip. News of Sylvester's death tells me otherwise. Scotty's *Enterprise* cannot come to my rescue; I can't reach out and touch my brother. The global village is only a theory; at this moment it is exposed as a lie. And I find myself forgetting, even resenting, all the good things I like about Raleigh; those things that have made Raleigh home. The State Farmers Market, for one. A place that gives me intense joy; that stirs warm feelings in me akin to the kiss one hurriedly steals from a new lover before rushing off. Seven years on and I still can't believe this market is open every day of the year! Driving to the State Farmers Market on Saturdays always fills me with anticipation of what I might find, besides fresh fruits and vegetables, once I get there. I have no illusions I'd find ethnic African foods. For such items, I go to specialty grocery stores or visit the summer produce stands at the flea market on Capital Boulevard. These alternative food outlets are far from my mind as anticipation grows once I turn left from Nazareth onto Centennial Parkway. As I drive closer to the market, I imagine throngs of people already busy shopping; people from all walks of life strolling from one stall to the next, some in pointless banter, some lingering to chat with the farmers about their produce even as other buyers wait patiently for their turn. I always smile when I turn left onto Centennial for the simple fact that were I in Cameroon, once I made that turn, I would have heard the market come alive, if not before. West African markets are boisterous venues where people interact with such emotional abandon you can hear the market from miles away. You can hear it beckoning, calling out to you, calling your name, inviting you to partake, even for a brief moment, in the joy of living on this planet. One hears African markets before seeing and experiencing their pulsating intoxication. A cacophony of voices ignites a rush and propels one's steps to this theater of human dramas. That is why I am always drawn to Building 4, the Truckers Building, tucked away at the far end of the Farmers Market, where produce is sold in bulk; where one can split a box of tomatoes with a total stranger. "Want to split?" "Sure." Nothing's more fun. This is also the go-to place for brown skins and immigrant faces. These faces lure me to Building 4 even when I don't need to buy in bulk. On Saturdays, as I make my way through a crowd of brown people from many walks of life, I secretly fixate on those faces from home. It is a common practice among immigrants to play this silent game. The blank stare that says you can pretend to be American all you want but I can tell

67

you are an African: your clothes, your hair, your walk, your bearing, that bone structure, those facial marks, the way you rotate that mango on the tips of your fingers, the way you squeeze that pineapple with your thumb, index and middle fingers . . . they all betray you. My ears reach for their voices; for the tone and the pitch. Voice. Language. Two things that give it away, arousing competing thoughts in my head. That Pidgin English is definitely West African, probably Liberian. That one is obviously Nigerian. Those francophones over there are definitely sub-Saharan Africa; they're probably Congolese. Those two are without a doubt Senegalese. I walk closer. Sometimes, I say, Hi. Sometimes I get a cheerful response; sometimes not. Sometimes I am engaged in a spirited conversation in which we compare notes about what country we are *originally* from and what the political climate is like *back there*. We chat about how long we've been here; we skillfully avoid the taboo question, *What do you do here?* But when one person volunteers they're here just biding their time, planning for when they'll return home, For Good, we burst into hysterical laughter, recognizing we've heard the same bullshit many many times before. You know that ten, twenty, thirty years later, you will bump into this going-home-for-good talker and you'd likely hear them say it all over again. We recognize this as our acknowledgment that despite the envy of all those we left back home; despite it all, immigration is experienced as a form of impoverishment. It is a state of mind that frames and defines an immigrant's relationship with their sense of place, their sense of belonging in America.

When I moved from Hattiesburg to Raleigh, my early interactions with Raleighites involved navigating a thorny insider-outsider minefield. People thought—and some flatly said it—that I was one of the many Katrina refugees who had fled the ravages of the monster to seek safety in North Carolina. I would see the disappointment in their faces when my reasons for coming here—a job at N.C. State—contradicted the authority of their pronouncement. When they got over the shock that I had spent eleven years of my life in Mississippi and, god forbid, seemed unfazed by their reaction, they would proceed with a nervous, sometimes mocking laugh, to tell me just how bad Mississippi was/is.

"Mississippi isn't as bad as you think."

"Ha! Girl, you don't *know* Mississippi," they'd say. "Mississippi? Mississippi? You spent how long in Mississippi? Are you for real? . . . Do you know what they did/do to black people? To people like you? I drove through Mississippi in the Seventies and couldn't wait to get out of that state . . . Mississippi is one motherfucker . . ."

"Like I said, you don't know Mississippi. Mississippi has changed a lot . . ."

"You're not from around here . . . Bless your heart . . ."

"Look, are there things in Mississippi that haven't changed? Sure. But Mississippi has also changed a lot and the rest of America hasn't changed with it."

"Honey, listen . . . you're not from around here. I can tell from your accent that you're not from here. Are you from Jamaica? I can tell you are from Jamaica . . ."

"Not really. I've been to Jamaica a number of times. Not a single Jamaican ever thought I am, could be Jamaican. They always knew I was from Africa. They didn't know what country, but they *knew*."

"I could have sworn you were from the islands. Being from Africa and all, that's why you think Mississippi is no bother."

"I didn't say that."

"So what are you saying, Shug?"

"I'm saying, like any other place in America, the land of Faulkner and Welty has changed. It is convenient for the rest of America to continue believing that nothing has changed in the Magnolia State. That way, you can always dump on them. You can always feel better about yourself by pointing the finger at Mississippi . . ."

"Honey, let me tell you something. Those people are some badass racists . . ."

It gets tiresome when people make every effort to impress upon me how lucky I am to have left that badass racist place for North

Carolina; for the Triangle, with its RTP and world-class colleges and universities where people are educated, liberal, and nice. This way of thinking is
a luxury they can afford; lucky they! They were not with me on Blue Ridge
Road when a police officer gave a ticket to the man who had rear-ended
my son's car and proceeded to tell the gentleman, right in front of me and
my son, how said gentleman could get out of the ticket he had just been
issued. My son, one of those young black males the media claims to know,
looked at me and me him. A look that my people, the Beba, would say was
as pregnant as a full moon. I've been profiled—oh, that dirty word—more
times in Raleigh than I was my entire eleven years in Mississippi. When
I came to Raleigh, I lived in an apartment for one year to give me time to
know the city, but more so, to determine where I'd want to buy a home.
My loan officer requested eighty percent of the mortgage loan from one
bank and ten percent, a home equity loan, from another. I had owned
a home in Hattiesburg's Oaks Historic District for ten years: a beautiful turn-of-the-twentieth-century, two-story Southern home, sporting
columns and walk-in closets; a home I still miss and could never afford in
Raleigh. When you come to America as an immigrant, when you've lived
in America for as long as I have and worked hard at embracing your root-
edness, something as simple as a mortgage application, as jarring as that
2am phone call, slaps complacency out of you replacing it with a feeling
that you might never truly be American no matter how hard you try. I was
not prepared for the treatment I got from the ten-percent-equity-loan bank.
I got a call from a bank representative who requested among other things
a photocopy of my passport. Why? She answered my question by telling
me the documents were needed to proceed any further with my application. Why do you need a photocopy of my passport? To proceed with your
loan application, she repeats. I can't for the sake of me see why you need
my passport. Are you or your bank USCIS? Can I speak to your supervisor? My supervisor isn't available at the moment, she tells me. I hung up
and tried to get over the shock of her request by reminding myself that

I had provided them with documentation about previous homeownership; that I had sold that home despite the housing bubble. That didn't seem to matter. I surmised that someone had seen a strange looking name—Juliana Makuchi Nfah-Abbenyi—and alarm bells went off. I was angry, to put it mildly, because I assumed they wouldn't ask an American for a photocopy of their passport. Even more, I was deeply saddened that this, and any such request, erased or chipped away at the oath of American citizenship I had proudly taken, under extreme difficult conditions, in Jackson, MS, two weeks after Katrina's eye made landfall in Mississippi and with one master stroke wiped out Pass Christian. I could have told this bank representative that when I bought my home, and without much fuss in Hattiesburg, I was then a Green Card–carrying Resident Alien; but I didn't. I could have told this bank representative that I am a U.S. citizen; but I didn't. I composed myself and called my loan officer. We'll take our business elsewhere, he said, and that was that.

I've realized while writing this piece that I cannot write about Raleigh, North Carolina, without recalling Hattiesburg, Mississippi. My first semester in a full-time tenure-track position at the University of Southern Mississippi ended with the news of the death of my sibling, the fifth of ten children, in Yaounde, Cameroon. A first. Unfamiliar territory. I was so traumatized by the death of my brother, Ezekiel Takumberh Nfah, that I locked myself in my apartment for an entire week, never stepping foot outside. I wrote "Mourning . . . in distant lands," a poem, part of which I've excerpted here that captured my raw emotions; that poked holes in my belief that I had made the right decision to come to America. I later used the poem to dedicate my book of short fiction, *Your Madness, Not Mine: Stories of Cameroon*, to my younger brother, Ezekiel.

Call me back in ten minutes
call me back
call me
ten minutes
ten
nine eight seven

CALL ME BACK
011 237 31 . . .
Hello
but, but, I only spoke with him
yesterday, this morning
WE talked about him
he was coming
HOME
next week, the doctors said.
New Year's at home, the doctors said.

How does one mourn?
How does one mourn in distant lands
holed up like a caged rat
hemmed in
barricaded behind cold friendless dreary cubic walls?

Day one
Day two
Day 3? Day 4? Day 5?
Sunrise? or sunset?
Mid-day? or mid-night?

. . .

Heard about your brother, they say
Died in some sort of freakish accident?
Call me
if you wish to talk
confined in my private jail
my ancestors, where are you?
when my tongue is tethered
when i am too weak to howl.

Are you mad?
You *don't ask*
you *come over*
you *sit with me*
you *hold my hand*
you *cuddle me*
you sing songs
we sing, we weep, we dance, we smile
we invoke them
And Taku reveals
he's at peace
how he loved life
how he almost cheated death
almost.

. . .

No, it was no freakish accident
a natural gas explosion blew away our tongues
cloaking us in silence
of what is said
of what is heard and left unsaid
shredding my insides paper thin
my gaping wounds left exposed

blood satiating choking
day 6? day 7? day 8?
one week?

74

I had never in my life felt so alone until I answered that 3am call in my Hattiesburg apartment on December 26, 1995. I have experienced a familiar helplessness with Rev. Sylvester's death; that is one ingredient a distant death never changes for an immigrant, but this time, I have not felt alone. I have not been alone. Flowers, calls, emails from friends and colleagues remind me of that fact; abundant gestures of concern and love from my children and family remind me I am not alone; members of the Triangle Cameroon Association holding a wake in my house on 03/15/13 to coincide with the wake in Cameroon remind me I am not alone. The crape myrtle I planted in Hattiesburg has sunk roots deep into Southern soil, has cultivated branches that adapt by bending in the wind yet outlasting the danger.

And so, the stories that have shaped my life and living revolve in a continuous loop between and within locations. When I wake to the sounds of early spring, I am reminded of the familiar sights, sounds and smells of mockingbirds, woodpeckers, swallows, cardinals, wrens, jays, azaleas, crape myrtles, gardenias, magnolias. When pollen blankets my car in Raleigh, I remember the much more copious amounts of pollen that clung to my car in south Mississippi. Two years ago, the U.N. Conference for Women came to N.C. State. I was on "The New South" panel with women who shared insights on immigration and the changing face of the South. When Regina Wang of the *News & Observer* interviewed me at the conclusion of the panel, I told her that "I hope it's a place where I can live and thrive, where I can bring something positive and receive something positive back." I used to obsess over what home is, what home means, where home is, but when I read Isidore Okpewho's foreword to my book, *The Sacred Door and Other Stories: Cameroon Folktales of the Beba*, I relented and learned to take comfort in his words: "Makuchi may lament . . . that leaving her native Beba home in Cameroon has removed her from the warm, familial environment in which the tales in her collection were originally told, or that she has not succeeded in recreating with her children the traditional context of cultural education in which she was raised. But she is bringing that education to a larger, universal audience that includes her own children here in North America who, in time, will come to recognize that—to paraphrase an old Igbo (Nigerian) proverb—'Where you mend the roof, there is your home.'"

JULIANA M. NFAH-ABBENYI is professor of English and Comparative Literature and director of Diversity Programs and Faculty/Staff Diversity in the College of Humanities and Social Sciences at North Carolina State University. She is the author of four books and many other publications. She writes fiction under the pen name Makuchi. "Woman of the Lake," her short story about the 1986 Lake Nyos disaster that wiped out entire communities in Cameroon, was nominated for the Pushcart Prize.

A World Apart

A Forest in the Middle of It

BETTY ADCOCK

IT WAS A LATE SUMMER SUNDAY sometime in the mid-1970s, and
I had been having a difficult time juggling motherhood, a job writing for an
advertising agency, part-time teaching, and trying to write my second book
of poetry. I was staying up half the night working on poems, then worry-
ing about all the things I wasn't taking care of, the usual things a young
too-busy parent worries about. My husband, Don, was a born optimist,
a jazz and classical flutist, and a director of music at N.C. State University
where he directed the symphonic band, the marching band, and the jazz
band, in addition to teaching lecture courses on the history of music,
jazz appreciation, and other subjects. We both worked very hard.

There is a kind of stress that can tear at the fabric of life, the ties of family,
and even the weave of selfhood. Such stress I think is more common now,
but in those days a woman working, especially at several different kinds of
work, was not the norm in a suburban south still hungover from the 1950s.
I would eventually find my way into a career I could stay with and love.

But not that year. Not that summer.

Don knew I was fraying. He had rare instincts for a man of his generation, and he knew exactly how to help me. "Come on," he said that Sunday morning, "I have something to show you."

Reedy Creek Park was then a well-kept secret in Wake County. It had been established in 1950 as a park for African Americans in Raleigh's still rigidly segregated society. It was designed to be the "other" version of William B. Umstead Park, which had opened as Crabtree Recreation Area in 1937. The two parks were contiguous. Together (there is much irony in their being together though apart) they comprised several thousand wooded acres surprisingly near the fast-growing capital city. In 1966, the two were combined into one park under the name William B. Umstead State Park. Those names tell us something about them. The one is a simple country name, a clear diagram of a place and its character. We see the reeds; we hear the tumbling of the creek in that name. By contrast, the main park, which now encompasses both land parcels, bears the name of a long dead politician who was a U.S. congressman, senator, and briefly governor of North Carolina. Even after the parks were consolidated, people kept the name Reedy Creek Park separate though officially it became only a second entrance to Umstead.

That summer Sunday when I was in my thirties, I knew nothing of all this. We'd always had our family gatherings at Umstead Park. There the WPA had built tables and small barbecue pits where we could build fires and roast hot dogs for picnics. I had never heard of Reedy Creek. My husband, however, was a runner, and he knew its pristine trails very well indeed. Even today the place is a runner's haven. Don was going to show me the woods in the middle of our city, on a then-graveled road just past the DMV and the pastures of N.C. State's animal husbandry farms.

We parked at the entrance, which was then closed to automobiles. The path in was wide and had once been wider. Wonderful edge-growth of pine saplings, some longleaf, and wild plum bushes had crept in and narrowed the way. Partway along was a marvelous tree, I think an oak, very large and old and taking a great chunk of the sky in its wide arms. It would play a role in a later day at the park. There were small plums on the bushes. Puddles from old rains marked the earth of the unkempt way, along with deer tracks. Tiny frogs animated the puddles, bringing memories of my east Texas childhood when I used to catch such new-limbed leapers and bring them home in a fruit jar full of creek water.

This whole place felt like home. I had grown up around such near-wild wandering fecundity, with acres of heavy woods around my childhood's homeplace. As we walked, holding hands, toward the spot where two smaller trails, one on either side, snaked off into the deep woods, Don and I listened for birds whose calls we'd later learn to recognize, accompanied briefly by the bells of Mount Olive Church pealing out a hymn, softened by distance into proper mystery.

That day we explored the right-hand trail, which led to a small rather overgrown lake. The forest was perfectly still but for the occasional bird cry or squirrel skitter. Coming back from the lake, we found a downed log just right for sitting on. Sun-dapple and leaf-crunch. Dark green moss on one side of our log gave off the pure deep scent of earth when I pressed a piece of it to my face. A fallen log nearby had taken a still-blooming sapling with it. Small white grubs appeared when I lifted a piece of loose bark from our deteriorating couch. All these things I kept as if in a treasure box, along with the rediscovery (I had always known it) that the great thing about a forest is the singular silence that lets you *hear*. In such quiet, just far enough from roads, every sound is an event—as water is for fish— in which we simply *are*, and are unmarked, who do not mark the time.

I came back to Reedy Creek countless times. Often with Don, but as often I came by myself, preferring early weekday mornings when I could be sure of being completely alone. Sometimes I brought my breakfast. I loved early light in the tall trees. I was never afraid. The park had a few hikers and runners and from time to time horseback riders, but not on weekday mornings. I owned the place then, the light, the carpet of leaves, the insects and blooming undergrowth, the sky etched with branches.

One day, as I dozed lying with my head on a log, I heard a rustling I took for early hikers; but then it became oddly disorganized, a different sound that was coming too close. I raised my head and found myself looking directly into the eyes of a very large deer, probably an eight- or ten-pointer, almost close enough to touch. I could see the individual hairs on the muzzle, the shine of his nose, and even color variations in the antlers. He stopped stock-still and we stared at each other. As long as I could, I held the gaze, but my neck was killing me. When I had to put my head down, he leapt into a turn and ran, flew with his white banner, vanished the way a shadow does in new light. One of my books has the poem I made of that day, titled "Revenant," a word meaning "spirit."

Once, Don and I lay in December leaves on a hillside marveling at how long the beech leaves stay after all other kinds have fallen. Suddenly we were watching five deer running hard together, right past us, a minor stampede spurred by something we couldn't see.

Another time we hiked eight miles on the Wilderness Trail that wound through heavy growth, steep hills, and other beautiful difficulties, a very long way for someone as unused to heavy exercise as I was. We almost had to stay the night in the woods because, as it got dark, we became unable to read the guiding white blazes on the trees. I was almost disappointed when we came out just at full dark onto the parking lot.

Sometimes we would leave the trails entirely and just wander around. Once we came upon a stand of daffodils, the heirloom kind, blooming bright yellow against tangles of low vines and forest duff. Looking further, we found a caved-in well, its set-stone sides dry and sculptural below ground. There were other signs that there'd been a farm, a family's life lit by these daffodils — still blooming after how many decades of abandonment? The oddly ruffled antique flowers showed up in a poem I wrote for our fiftieth wedding anniversary.

For years, I visited those trails less traveled by when I was worn down, when I was saddened by loss, or extremely happy, or just as a matter of habit. Once an indigo bunting, that bright rarity, flew from low sapling to sapling at eye level just ahead of me, staying with me the whole length of the entrance trail, a guide made somehow of sky.

Still another memory lodges in the branches of the great tree we'd pass on the entrance trail. On one of my solitary visits I was stopped still by the softly loud fluttering of a huge flock of cedar waxwings gathered in a quiet bustling among turning autumn leaves. I watched that confounding of feather and leaf for several minutes before the birds rose all together in a chorus of high, clear single notes.

I haven't been to what I thought of as *my* woods in many years. More people found out about the place for one thing. Then age made me less able to navigate any kind of trail, having brought two knee replacements. And my husband, who had something to show me one Sunday long ago, died two summers past. I can hope Reedy Creek has stayed a little more hidden than most parks. Perhaps it has not been utterly altered to suit the habits of those who like convenience more than brambles, community rather than solitude. I'm guessing that Reedy Creek keeps something of the wild spirit, its deer and migrating flocks, its graceful silence, and the wildflowers we learned to identify, goat's rue, butterfly weed, and wild pea among them, edging the ever-narrowing main path, and wood sorrel, cross vine, and trillium among the trees.

When our daughter was a cash-strapped college student, her birthday gift to me one year was to bring me to Reedy Creek. We sat together on a log in the busy, shadowed silence while she read aloud one of Sarah Orne Jewett's lovely stories powered by the natural world, a world available to us even here, because there was a forest in the middle of Raleigh.

BETTY ADCOCK is the author of six volumes of poetry, most recently *Slantwise*. Her poems have appeared in many anthologies, including three Pushcart Prize collections. She is the recipient of the North Carolina Award for Literature, the Hanes Award from the Fellowship of Southern Writers, the Poet's Prize, and other awards and honors. She was writer-in-residence at Meredith College for twenty years and a visiting professor at North Carolina State University. She is a member of the faculty of the Warren Wilson College MFA program for writers.

Fox View, Montclair Neighborhood

ELAINE NEIL ORR

Across clearings, an eye,
A widening deepening greenness,
Brilliantly, concentratedly.
Coming about its own business.
  —Ted Hughes, "The Thought-Fox"

MAY 28, 2012. I turn the manuscript over to my editor. I enter a lull. Mornings I sleep until eight, drink green tea until ten, dress by noon, at which point I am ready to sit on the back porch and watch the songbirds. A week later and it's June, unseasonably cool for Raleigh, and the birds still dance at midday. Two male cardinals vie for space between the fence and hedgerow. A chipmunk runs down the sidewalk, freezes for a moment, takes me for myself or a piece of furniture, darts past. It's time to turn to afternoon tea: iced with lemon. I put on the teapot. Before long, I will eat a pimento cheese sandwich. Not much later and I will stretch out on the lime-green couch in the living room.

Our house sits on a hillock, a corner lot providing a view of the neighborhood. The front yard is deep and wide, the backyard abbreviated into one corner of the square-ish third of an acre. *Montclair* our neighborhood is called, behind the more famed and increasingly sought-after North Hills. We remain a little ragged around the edges, these homes built in the early to mid-1960s.

The malaise continues for days. Symptoms include the need to sleep every two hours. Even eating tires me. So does talk. I avoid the telephone. I ache down through muscle into bone. When I stand I feel faint and have to sit again. The hint of a sore throat presents itself when I swallow. A fullness dips into my chest, sensations portending a summer cold. But nothing develops. Instead, these are constant sensations of deep exhaustion. The end of the teaching year at N.C. State, six years of writing this book, the ongoing tightrope I walk as a transplant patient. If I push against this state of being, I develop a slight nausea.

Recline. Rest. This may take weeks.

I am protective of our split-level, a feeling almost primitive, as an animal might experience when its territory is being invaded, trees cut, fields shorn, creeks rerouted. Not far from us, other split-levels are being torn down and replaced by newer, larger homes. This advancement is an offshoot of the renewed North Hills. What I am talking about is basic shelter.

One afternoon I wake from a nap, sit up, gaze out the window into the backyard. An awfully large cat has entered our songbird paradise. I watch as it circles the base of a tree. Moving to the window, I see my mistake. Not feline but canine: gray fox, snout and tail and heavily bristled back;

the ends of the fur dark; inner fur a lighter gray; dark streak down the back and along the top of the tail; rusty orange along its neck and hind legs. Wild. For a moment I am too astonished to react. *My languid hours, his silent stalking. And the fox is here in my yard, ringing round the pine tree's base, his nose now here, now here, now.*

No!

By the time I slam out the back door, the fox is gone. The neighbor's cat, arched like a moon, sidesteps backwards. So I saved her, I think. And just then I see the fox, the comma shape of mouse or chipmunk in his maw. Delicately he retreats, quiet as midnight, tail down, the yard now blank and blazing in the sun. Too late and yet I take off barefooted, awkward, and limping across bramble and pine cone. "No," I cry, waving my arms like a lame bird.

Gray foxes are native to North Carolina while the red fox was brought by the British. In spite of hunting and trapping and urbanization, gray fox is probably as common in the state today as it has been over the past million years, trapping small prey, but also foraging on berries, peanuts, and corn. And anything we humans leave around in our Raleigh yards and streets: an apple core dropped, the cat food, a teenager's lunch remnants tossed out a car window. An adult gray fox is nine to eleven pounds, about three to three and a half feet from nose to tip of the tail.

There are things I have not told yet that lead to this malaise. These are the harder things. A misunderstanding with a friend that goes on for months. We are both stubborn as old captains. My ninety-two-year-old mother who needs me every day now. "Everyone has left," she says over the phone. I am stretched out on the couch. Her voice pleads. "Where have they gone?" I say. "Isn't it a holiday?" she says. "No," I say. "Well, they've gone somewhere," she reports from her apartment at Magnolia Glen on Creed-moor Road. I wonder if she means not her co-dwellers, but her husband, my father, her college friends—all dead, six of her seven brothers and sisters gone. She wants my attention. I am too tired. It weighs on me, her need for a different kind of shelter.

A fox's home range might be a square mile or less and the fox may spend its entire life in this small range. The gray fox seeks brushy woodlands and hardwood forests, is generally nocturnal in its roaming, and chooses its den location based on proximity to water. The den might be a hollow in logs and tree trunks, crevices between and under rock, a space the fox and its mate will line with grass, leaves, or shredded bark. Our split-level on the hillock in Montclair is within one hundred yards of a creek. I've tried to follow that creek. It goes down along Wimbledon, which Collingswood Drive (our street) intersects, coursing gently through front yards. In some yards, it disappears into a huge pipe and comes out the other side, into the next yard. And then somewhere in the curve of the road, it disappears. I've thought of cutting through yards, trying to find where the creek goes. Wimbledon comes out to Shelley Road and the last three blocks of Shelley decline steeply, coming to the larger creek that flows out of Shelley Lake and ripples along the greenway. So our creek must link up with it. But how and where I don't know.

"Who will you eat dinner with?" I say to my mother. "Oh, Dot is gone," she says. I wait. "Are there other friends you can join?" I say at last. "Well, the other three are here," she says, meaning the other three women she usually dines with. So only one friend is gone but she feels everyone is gone. "Oh good," I say. "I'll call you again this evening." She seems better now. We can end the call. I turn over, pull up the white afghan, sleep.

The fox comes back one midmorning. I am on my usual schedule in this lull. I spy him out the window that looks onto our enormous fan of a front yard. He stands in the middle of the road but turns, looking over his shoulder, back in my direction. I call my husband. "Look," I say, "the fox." "Where?" he says. "There," I say, pointing. We stand close to one another, looking out. The fox circles, comes onto our lawn. We walk out the front door. The fox is unfazed, though even the most domesticated dog would have reacted to us by now. In a moment, he trots over to the neighbor's yard across the street. "That's a bold fox," my husband says. A few minutes later, rinsing the dishes, I catch a glimpse of the fox out the kitchen window. "There he goes again," I say. He makes a path just where I saw him before, alongside the hedgerow. Then he is gone and we don't see him again that day. Only later do I consider how he must have circled our house, only later learn that gray foxes climb trees, can jump from limb to limb with ease, have occasionally been spotted sleeping in owl or hawk nests.

Time passes. July 8. It's sixty-seven degrees at nine a.m. I shiver on the porch in my pajamas. A sweater would help but I am too indifferent to re-enter the house, climb the stairs, and retrieve it. I nibble on a breakfast of aged cheddar cheese and sliced avocado. A bright towhee lands on the back lawn. Members of the wren family that had a nest atop an upturned broom on our carport flit from pine to shrub and back. Light falling through leaves angles into the yard. A chipmunk comes running down the path, sees me, skedaddles into the grass, over to the fence and along it. From where I sit, I view larger oaks, two variations of pine, a pecan tree, a maple. Here appears a tiny young bird in the grass, its markings so indistinct, I don't recognize its kind. A toady mushroom has sprouted in the night.

Gray foxes breed between mid-February and late March. Gestation takes about seven and a half weeks. When the kits are young, the male will hunt for the female, who remains in the den, which is why I call this fox *He*. This time of year the kits are likely still in the den with the mother. The father is hunting by day and by night, and our cul-de-sac, a relatively quiet neighborhood, with many old trees, overgrown backyards, near greenway and a creek, is a promising area from the fox's point of view. In our bird feeder we leave a mixture that includes berries and nuts, which the fox will eat if he misses the bird.

My back aches. Otherwise I feel fine until I begin to move toward a project, say cleaning out a closet or organizing my books. Immediately I feel the revolt, dizziness, a sense of weight, a resounding "no" from the body. I remain on the porch, feet cool on the concrete slab.

A cardinal lands, pecks among the pine straw, then sunbathes.

Approaching ten o'clock, the air is still cool.

At two thirty, the backyard itself is in a lull and it's only eighty degrees. My eyes shift to the shining high oak leaves on the other side of the neighbor's house. A small flying insect of some sort has hatched by the hundreds and darts about three feet above the grass, looking like spits of snow. Suddenly a wind rustles the day, tender against my skin, and I recall bodily pleasure but only as memory.

A week later I begin reading a novel, my first intellectual activity in weeks. I make a good start. It's a fine novel, a little discouraging because the life of the primary character is discouraging. And this condition of life seems not about to change for him. I keep at it, at least a chapter a day. I get halfway through and then leave the book on the coffee table. Several times I pick it up but do not read. I sit on the back porch instead, even at ninety-five degrees. Summer has finally arrived with a vengeance. Midafternoon the sun begins its decline. I focus on the hedge, the one the fox trots by. My vision goes hazy. My brain begins to rest. This is more than physical rest. It feels as though the curves of my gray matter are unfolding from a long tightness, unfurling like fern. The sensation is lovely. I wonder if I've ever felt it before. The neighbor's yellow-green lawn shimmers through open spaces in the hedge.

Like other canines, the fox has red-dominated retinas and sees better in the dark than humans do. His vision is dichromatic, meaning he can pick out two colors: blue and yellow, and shades of gray. He uses other clues to see: smell and sound primarily. His eyes, set at a twenty-degree angle, increase peripheral vision but compromise his binocular vision (which humans have—the field of view of each eye overlapping). His depth perception is less acute unless he looks straight ahead, which is just how he does look in jumping, leaping, catching. He also has less visual acuity than a human and must be within twenty feet to see me as well as I can see him at seventy feet. Motion sensitivity is the critical aspect of his vision. Is this why the fox turned his head when my husband and I stepped out the door? He heard sound and saw motion.

The third time I am on the back porch talking on the phone with a friend. It's eleven a.m. My friend and I are both tired. If we aren't careful we will try to outdo each other with our complaints. The day is bright, though I am sheltered so that anyone looking from the neighbor's yard would see me, if at all, as a figure in a hollow: the bright surround of daylight and me in deep shadow as of a cave.

I glance up and there is the fox, sitting, staring, twenty feet away, just there at the break in the hedgerow, where he could, in the dark of night, make a choice: this way behind the hedgerow, or this way through the yard.

Did he smell me first and then see me? Does he see me yet?

"There's my fox," I say to my friend on the phone, just above a whisper. I am almost as startled as I was the first time. Startled by his presence, his calm, his gaze. I try to explain to my friend, keeping my voice low: "This fox. I've been seeing this fox; he's been coming through our yard." I try not to move. "How exciting," she says. "A good omen." *Exactly*, I think, which is why I don't want him to move. For now, he sits with the patient, regal demeanor of a cat, peering and peerless. What happens next? Perhaps I look away and when I look back he is gone. I keep watching for him all that day but he doesn't show himself.

Why do I desire the fox? Killer of birds, a chipmunk's beating heart laid open. *Imagine him stepping silently into the road, looking back over his shoulder. Moving across my lily bed, he licks water from a leaf. He ambles near the coneflower; a spore attaches itself to his tail. Later it falls near our creek, a stretch where sunlight hits. Next season, it germinates. By July the pink flower blooms. Just so, our Raleigh neighborhood — if we can keep it a little ragged; if all the split-levels are not cut down and all the trees with them — we remain an ecosystem. We haven't yet destroyed all natural means of distributing seed and sustenance, even though with these new houses, nothing appears to happen naturally. The entire lot is shorn. Every blooming thing — dogwood, azalea, iris — cleared out so that rolls of grass can be laid once the house is built. To the fox's eye and nose such a space is neutered.*

Aug. 28. We have come through a season of limp gray skies, warm temperatures, and rain into mild sunny days of late summer, temperatures in the sixties in the morning, sunlight filling the morning, every color of the outdoors heightened.

I seem miraculously healed, waking with energy and desire, thinking— "What will I find today? What can I do?" I experience that deep pleasure that comes with interest in my own life, in what I will create. Our neighbor has acquired a rooster and chickens. Now we hear a rooster in the morning. We also hear him mid-day and evening. Lie down for a nap and I am sure to be awakened by the rooster. The chickens cluck. I can hear them moving about on the other side of the fence. It's a tall, solid fence, so we can't see into the yard. I imagine, grinning to myself, that they are free-range (good for them), and part of our somewhat haphazard, less-than-scrubbed-and-polished neighborhood. At first I imagine they will be safe from the fox next spring but then I remember that foxes can climb and jump.

My mother calls. I ask her how she is doing. "I'm not doing very well," she says. When I ask what's wrong, she tells me that she doesn't have any energy. She doesn't feel like doing anything. "I need to ask my doctor about it," she says. "Surely I'm not going to feel like this the rest of my life." "You won't," I say, hoping for her. "Remember, you had that long day Sunday, going to church and then to lunch with friends, and then that musical program in the afternoon at Pullen Baptist. After a day like that, your body has to recover." She doesn't answer directly. "It's such an artificial life," she says. I don't have a clue what she means. "Eating dinner and then coming back here to sit through the evening," she says. I haven't heard her say this before. She has been largely content in her living. When I asked her about moving in with me after my father died, she graciously declined. "Can you take a walk with a friend after dinner?" I say. And add: "I could come over some evenings." "You have things to do," she says. She is right, of course. My semester is started up. Like the fox, I'm on a schedule. She is beyond schedules. I have rested and rebounded. She may have some more energetic days but in general, her slope is downward. "I can come walk with you," I say, "at least once a week." She would like more.

Gray foxes inhabit all parts of North Carolina, from the Outer Banks to the Appalachians. Even as coyotes expand their range and displace the red fox, the gray fox holds its own. Is it this species' ability to climb that helps it survive a coyote's stalking? Folklore has favored the red fox for cunning, but the smaller gray fox is surviving better against intrusion, the human factor, the larger canine factor.

After years of debating and deferring and sometimes arguing over it, my husband and I have decided, against a realtor's recommendation ("Why not sell your house and buy one that already suits your needs?" —apparently split-levels, even near North Hills, are not ever going to become fashionable again) to remodel our house. We are staying put in our Sixties suburban dwelling with the small bathrooms and narrow hallway, three bedrooms squeezed together in the upper level, a room that will never escape the nomenclature of "den," and a carport rather than a garage. We are within reach of what we need: the greenway and a grocery store, shaded groves and the airport, open sky and my husband's office, bluebirds and Peking Garden Restaurant.

I haven't seen the fox for weeks. My husband saw him one more time, trotting his line behind the house, on the other side of the hedgerow. I was disappointed that I had not been chosen to see him that last time, as if some divine spirit had been choreographing these "chance" meetings and had somehow erred at the last. Surely the kits have now matured and he is not required to hunt as often. It's doubtful the fox and his mate have moved to another location. They generally remain put so long as food and water and shelter are adequate. They mate for life.

I won't see the fox until next year and only then if I am exhausted enough to be required to sit on my back porch for a month of mornings.

If the fox were writing this essay, he would report more sightings of me than I of him. But he would take less interest. I am only a slow and occasional inconvenience. His interest is elsewhere and his knowledge of Montclair is both more complex and more complete than mine. He knows it better than the realtor, better than the children who play basketball in the cul de sac. Human dwellers see separate yards. He sees zones of safe passage. We see surfaces. He sees in the dark. We enter our dens at night. He leaves his. We are surprised to hear the ripple of the creek. His ear perks to know its depth and coolness after a rain. He passes easily through a bed of poison ivy, maneuvers over or under oddly angled fallen trees left in backyards, knows in his certain, steady trot just where our creek intersects with the larger creek on the greenway. He knows the habits of the birds, and the habits of the large, unfurred mammals who periodically and unwittingly feed him. He walks by the moon and slips, knowing everything, at the edge of my perception.

ELAINE NEIL ORR is the author of a novel, A Different Sun; a memoir, Gods of Noonday: A White Girl's African Life (a Book Sense Top-10 Selection), and two books of literary criticism. She is on the faculty in English at North Carolina State University. Her memoirs and short fiction appear widely in such journals as the Missouri Review, Shenandoah, Image, Blackbird, and Memoir Journal.

Street Scenes

Autumn Prayer, North Carolina State

DORIANNE LAUX

When I walk to my car I see him
kneeling on a square of dirt beneath a tree,
his forehead pressed against a patch of gray grass.
I know he's praying so I walk lightly, respectfully,
my head down so he won't think I'm looking at him.
He's maybe 23, thin and kempt,
his black jeans and white shirt clean, pressed.
Cars roll by, students chat into cell phones.
No one seems to notice there's a young man praying.

When I get home I look up Muslim prayer times
on The Islamic Finder: Late Afternoon: Asr:
Immediately after the last time limit of Dhuhr
until sunset. He must do this all day,

no matter where he is, search for spots of earth

between classes, before work, after work,

like this one, maybe three square feet

beneath a young crape myrtle, native

to the Indian subcontinent, third largest

Muslim nation, with bark that changes color

and produces flowers of many different hues,

from deep purple to red to white with every shade

between, member of the loosestrife family

blessed with simple, ovoid, lustrous, thin-veined leaves

which release an aromatic odor when bruised,

and sets free, in autumn,

thousands of small winged seeds.

DORIANNE LAUX'S most recent collections are *The Book of Men,* winner of the Paterson Prize and the Roanoke-Chowan Award for Poetry, and *Facts about the Moon,* recipient of the Oregon Book Award. Coauthor of *The Poet's Companion: A Guide to the Pleasures of Writing Poetry,* she's recipient of fellowships from the National Endowment for the Arts and the Guggenheim Foundation. She teaches poetry in the creative writing program at North Carolina State University.

The Parade

An excerpt from Adam's Gift

JIMMY CREECH

AUTHOR'S NOTE: As a pastor, I was visited one day in 1984 by a parishioner named Adam. I'd known him quite a while. He had come to tell me that he was gay and was leaving The United Methodist Church, which refused to ordain "practicing homosexuals." That conversation set me on a life-long journey to end discrimination against gays and lesbians.

IN JUNE OF 1987, I moved . . . to Raleigh to be the pastor of Fairmont United Methodist Church. . . . I was glad to return to Raleigh, which had been my home from 1970 to 1973 when I was an associate pastor at Edenton Street United Methodist Church following my graduation from Duke Divinity School. The Fairmont church, a congregation of about seven hundred members located just two blocks from the campus of North Carolina State University, offered exciting opportunities and challenges for ministry. . . .

The congregation . . . graciously welcomed me as its pastor and I immediately felt at home. . . . Each Sunday, a large number of college students attended worship and I found their energy and openness to be stimulating.

Beyond the congregation, I became active in community efforts to end homelessness and oppose the U.S.-sponsored Contras in the war in Nicaragua. The first year at Fairmont went smoothly with lots of support from the congregation. I couldn't have been happier in my ministry.

Since Adam had awakened me to the church's persecution of lesbian, gay, and bisexual persons three years earlier, I had come to understand and accept sexual orientation as an essential, normal, and natural aspect of the human personality, regardless of whether its orientation was other-, both-, or same-gender orientation. I believed The United Methodist Church's policies and teachings about homosexuality were expressions of bigotry, comparable to racism.

102

In September of my first year at Fairmont, I accepted an invitation from Nancy Keppel [a lay minister in the United Church of Christ] to attend a meeting of clergy who wanted to discuss what could be done to end the mistreatment of gay people, especially by churches. . . .

It took several meetings and lots of discussion about what to do and how to do it, but ultimately we created the Raleigh Religious Network for Gay and Lesbian Equality (RRNGLE), originally composed of about fifteen pastors and lay persons from Episcopal, Roman Catholic, Lutheran, Presbyterian, Unitarian Universalist, United Church of Christ, Baptist, Metropolitan Community, and United Methodist churches, along with the rabbi of Raleigh's reform Jewish congregation. Our goal was to do educational work in the religious communities and in secular settings. We were committed to bearing public witness against discrimination, believing there was no integrity in offering support to gay people in the privacy of our offices but not in public arenas. In early 1988, I was chosen to be the convenor of RRNGLE, a position I would hold for the next two years.

The 1988 North Carolina Gay Pride Weekend was scheduled to take place in Raleigh in June, and RRNGLE was concerned that clergy in the local churches might use the event as an opportunity for gay bashing. In the hope of preventing that, we sent a letter to all clergy in the county, urging them to be sensitive to the fact that every congregation has members who are gay and members who are parents or siblings of gay persons. Since this was our first official correspondence, we created a letterhead with the names of all RRNGLE members printed down the left side of the page. As the convenor, I signed the letter and used the Fairmont church address and telephone number on the letterhead in case anyone wanted to respond.

A small RRNGLE delegation was to walk in the Pride March, one of the Gay Pride Weekend events. On Friday evening, the day before the march, Sarah Hitchcock, chairperson of Fairmont's Pastor-Parish Relations Committee, called to tell me that a copy of RRNGLE's letter to the area's clergy had been sent to the Wesley Bible Class—a Sunday school class of older men—by a local United Methodist minister, and that for the last two or three Sundays the letter had been the main topic of discussion. Sarah told me the class was preparing a resolution condemning the practice of homosexuality and anyone supporting homosexuals, which would be presented to me before worship on Sunday morning.

"Are you going to be in the gay pride march tomorrow?" Sarah asked. "Yes," I answered, "I will be walking with RRNGLE." While she assured me she supported what I was doing, she wanted me to understand that others did not. Sarah's call alarmed me, and for the first time, I felt anxious about how my work with RRNGLE might adversely affect my relationship with the Fairmont congregation. I had known this time would ultimately come because of the controversy over homosexuality in the church. I also knew that the emancipation of gay people from discrimination and violence was a just and necessary cause, and that no social change happens without resistance and conflict. So, though I felt anxious that night, I was determined to follow through with the march and with my work with RRNGLE.

The next day, I stood on the curb on Hillsborough Street with the Reverend Jim Lewis, director of Christian Social Ministries for the North Carolina Episcopal Diocese, and the Reverend Mahan Siler, pastor of Pullen Memorial Baptist Church, holding our new RRNGLE banner. It was a gorgeous June morning. The sun was unusually hot for so early in the day, and the sky was a bold Carolina blue with a few scattered, fluffy clouds. Already the atmosphere was exuberant. Lesbians and gay men, bisexual and transgender people, and their friends and families were all in a festive mood. Laughter and loud, cheerful voices filled the air.

As I watched the parade forming and moving along the street, a shiver of dread passed over me, like the shadow of a cloud riding a summer breeze. I knew walking in the march would be an irreversible act, and my life wouldn't be the same afterward. Not by chance, Charles Holland drove by in his red pickup truck. Our eyes met, and he quickly looked away. He was the scout for the Wesley Bible Class, come to confirm their suspicions about my actions.

104

My stomach churned as apprehension contended with compulsion, but I finally stepped off the curb to join the march. I was quickly swept up by the festivity, and my dread was dissolved by the energy of the crowd. Pink and lavender balloons filled the air. People carried banners and placards, and wore T-shirts, buttons, and sashes with slogans proclaiming gay pride. The rainbow symbol was everywhere, affirming diversity and unity. Male couples and female couples walked together, unashamedly holding hands and occasionally kissing. A lesbian marching band somewhere up in front established the rhythm and tempo for us to follow.

The march stretched for blocks. On the crest of the hills, I strained to see its beginning and end, but both were too far away. The estimated number of participants—from three to five thousand—was, for North Carolina in 1988, an amazingly large gathering for a gay pride march.

Walking immediately ahead of us was the Raleigh chapter of PFLAG. Thinking this must be a Polish gay rights organization, I asked one of the people holding the PFLAG banner about the group. She explained it was Parents, Family, and Friends of Lesbians and Gays, a proud gathering of mothers and fathers, sisters and brothers, sons and daughters, grandparents, aunts and uncles. I was moved by their courageous public display of unconditional love and acceptance of the gay people in their lives, in spite of the hostile climate in Raleigh.

Just behind us, members of St. John's Metropolitan Community Church pulled a little red wagon carrying a boom box playing familiar hymns — "Jesus Loves Me, This I Know," "Blessed Assurance, Jesus Is Mine," and "Just as I Am, Without One Plea." They sang as they walked, transforming the songs of private piety into profound public affirmations of a faith in God's radically unconditional love and acceptance. These lesbian, gay, transgender, and bisexual people had every reason to turn their backs on the church because they had been condemned, rejected, and vilified in the name of God and Jesus. But they were not just singing, they were testifying:

> Just as I am, without one plea,
>
> But that thy blood was shed for me,
>
> And that thou bidst me come to thee,
>
> O Lamb of God, I come, I come!
>
> Just as I am, though tossed about,
>
> With many a conflict, many a doubt,
>
> Fightings and fears within, without,
>
> O Lamb of God, I come, I come!

What I heard in these brave voices was a refusal to identify the rejection by the Christian church with the heart and mind of God. I heard them claim that they, too, were children of a loving God who had blessed them with innate dignity and integrity. The traditional church might have cast them out, but these faithful people knew that God had not and would not.

As we walked down Hillsborough Street toward downtown Raleigh, we passed several churches, their doors locked and windows dark. There was no acknowledgment of the march by the people who would gather in those churches the next morning.

Two young men followed beside us on the sidewalk, both dressed in white shirts and black slacks. One carried on his shoulder a large wooden cross with small wheels on the long end, allowing it to roll while creating the illusion that he bore a great burden. The other man, shaking a large, floppy, black leather Bible above his head, harangued us, spitting out, "Homosexuality is an abomination! Repent or be damned to the eternal fires of hell!"

On that Saturday morning, God was not in the hateful words of the men with the cross and Bible or in the empty churches. God was in the mass of proud and beautiful people on Hillsborough Street. God was the pride, dignity, and integrity that were being celebrated. God was the unconditional love that empowered the courage of PFLAG and the members of St. John's Metropolitan Community Church.

Walking in the 1988 Gay Pride March was no big deal in many respects. Yet, it profoundly affected and defined the rest of my life. The intellectual inquiry into issues affecting gay people that Adam had started me on . . . became that day walking down Raleigh's Hillsborough Street an existential passion for me. God's spirit—free from the small, cramped boxes of petty theological and cultural convention—was leading and moving within this flow of humanity, breathing life, energy, and hope into its shared vision for a just world in which freedom, equality, and peace for all people are real.

JIMMY CREECH was an ordained minister in The United Methodist Church for twenty-nine years. In 1999, he was found guilty of disobedience in a church trial and his credentials of ordination were withdrawn because he conducted a marriage ceremony for two men. He and his wife, Chris Weedy, live in Boylan Heights, one of Raleigh's historic neighborhoods. He is the author of *Adam's Gift: A Memoir of a Pastor's Calling to Defy the Church's Persecution of Lesbians and Gays.*

North State

DAVID RIGSBEE

My father came to me in a dream
to walk with me around a stadium.
Not wearing the jaunty motley of his last months:
the patchwork newsboy cap and paneled shirt
he wore when tearing around town,
smoke streaming from the car window.
"I'm not gonna make it," he said.
"This may be the last time.
I don't have the breath for it."
We cried and smiled all at once.
The apparition faded, and I lapped the spot
before I knew. That morning
I had stopped to take some pictures
of a new structure: a five-story globe
affixed to a museum headquarters.
It was Sunday, the crews were gone,
but the wooden scaffolding clung

to the girders, "North State Steel"
spray-painted on each rib.
I had come before the planks were taken away
like crosshatching erased,
before the world was made,
the panels bolted in place and painted
that planetary blue of earth from space,
that pendant marble
on which everything is always lost
like a glass eye that never sees
what it never ceases to watch.

DAVID RIGSBEE is the author, most recently, of *School of the Americas* (2012), *The Pilot House* (2011), and *The Red Tower: New and Selected Poems* (2010). He has been the recipient of numerous fellowships and awards, including the Oscar Young Award for the best poetry book by a North Carolina author, the Sam Ragan Award for contributions to the arts in North Carolina, and a Pushcart Prize.

Go Pack

TINA HAVER CURRIN

THE FIRST TIME I VISITED RALEIGH, I was twelve years old and got stuck under my stepsister's waterbed. Hers was a bed for the particularly messy, with dark, wooden panels to lift the mattress and create ample storage along the sides and underneath. The foot of the frame was equipped with a little ligneous door to hide the mess, and a tiny pin-tumbler lock to keep it from creeping out. As such, cleaning Caroline's room usually consisted of stuffing stray items into the under-bed vault and latching the door. Which meant, of course, that it was a precarious event any time she needed to get something out.

"Tina, hurry up and get your chicken ass in there," she ordered. "We need to find that tape." On this day she stood, shoulders squared, next to the bed, addressing me with a firm point toward the small door.

Even though we were both twelve, I knew that Caroline was the dominant one in our relationship. She had strong features and an even stronger voice; she was beginning to look like a woman, while I was still a wisp of angular bones with several stubborn baby teeth left. The change became clear at Christmas, during the week that I visited Raleigh on a family vacation. Caroline's mom, Lisa, was a graduate of North Carolina State University, and wanted us to see the 115-foot, Romanesque bell tower that stood proudly atop a grassy square on her alma mater's campus. It was like a sentry, she said, standing guard over the university, and it was important we see it.

"It looks like a fat toothpick," I replied, looking at the bell tower through the backseat window as we drove by. I wasn't particularly impressed. As Lisa tried to turn around and face me, she jerked the car strongly to the left, forcing me to fall sideways into Caroline.

"Ugh, get off me!" my stepsister screamed, pushing me away. I stuck my tongue out at her, and then scooted over. Without warning, Caroline reached across the seat and punched me in the arm, making me yelp.

"Ow! Dad, help!" My bicep began to throb. I cradled it against my chest. "Dad, she punched me!" Caroline looked at me and shrugged, as though nothing had happened.

"Stop it. Both of you."

I could tell Lisa was frustrated. She wanted to take a few family pictures in front of the bell tower, so we all sat silently in the car, making an uncomfortably slow creep through campus in search of metered parking. When we found a parking deck, we started making dizzying circles upward in search of the summit, and crested the final loop eight laps later. On the open patio of the top floor, the sky formed a giant, gray dome above us. The clouds stretched up and over, enveloping the campus in a kind of silvery winter bubble. I had never seen anything like it back home in Florida. Would there be snow? I asked.

"Snow comes to Raleigh once every ten years," Lisa said curtly. "So no."

"I thought this was *North* Carolina," I snapped. Didn't it always snow in the north? I heard my dad sigh from the passenger's seat, so I shut up.

We got out of the car and walked toward Hillsborough Street, the university's obligatory college strip, in search of pizza. Our parents pulled us past several gift shops, but something caught Caroline's eye. Suddenly, she asked me for a Christmas present: a shirt with the word FOXY across the chest in flirtatious felt letters. My mom, completely unaware of the fact that my social position was growing increasingly omega, had sent me to Raleigh with a $10 McDonald's gift certificate for Caroline instead. Not to mention that the word FOXY freaked me out, and the bright, soft letters across the chest almost begged to be touched with the timid caress of an adolescent finger. I ignored Caroline's request and asked my dad where we were in the ten-year snow cycle. Wasn't there a chance that this was year ten?

But Lisa was right. It stayed dry. After a few minutes, we came across a bookstore with a giant triangular sign jutting out from the building like an old movie theater marquee. The windows were covered with dozens of anthropomorphic wolves, all wearing tiny sailor's caps, turtleneck sweaters, and no pants. Their sweaters were emblazoned with the N.C. State logo. It reminded me of the childish symbol I used to draw on my notebooks in elementary school—two pairs of three notched lines connected to make an S. How dumb, I thought. But Caroline was enticed by a T-shirt in the glass display, so we went inside. I waited near the door.

Most of the window wolves were dancing and playing football. A few particularly deranged ones were grilling up an enemy mascot, tossing their sailor-capped heads back with maniacal laughter. There were boy wolves and lady wolves. They all wore those stupid sweaters. GO PACK, the marquee announced.

"What's with all the wolves?" I asked the lanky kid at the register, who was dressed to the nines in red and white.

"We're the N.C. State *Wolfpack*!" he answered, tapping his thumb, middle, and ring fingers together to create a little hand sign that, I suppose, looked like a wolf. "Arroooo!"

"Arroooo!" Lisa echoed from somewhere within the shop.

Caroline had her eyes set on a bright red T-shirt that boldly proclaimed, GO TO HELL, CAROLINA, in capital letters. I didn't really know what it meant. But it had a curse word on it, so it was no wonder that it appealed to my stepsister.

"You sure do like shirts," I said as she walked up to the register. "Why do you want something that says Carolina should go to hell? Aren't we in Carolina? Or do they mean South Carolina?" I stared at the thing, puzzled.

Caroline rolled her eyes, and then turned toward her mother. "May I?" she asked. Without a word, Lisa hashed out a twenty from her purse.

"I don't get it," I said. "What's wrong with North Carolina?"

"It's complicated," Lisa sighed. "Would you like anything?" I looked around, not daring to venture too far from my post. There was a little key-chain next to the register, so I said I would take that, I guess, if it got us out of there more quickly.

When we got home, we all sat around the Christmas tree, and I gave Caroline the McDonald's gift certificate. I was more obsessed with the nine-foot-tall Fraser fir—a sappy, smelly thing cut from the woods nearby—than all the brightly wrapped presents that sat beneath it. The iridescent, woody plant was foreign to me; I was from the Gulf side of Florida, and the only Christmas trees I had ever seen were unnaturally green and made of plastic with the lights already installed.

Caroline wasn't at all charmed by my gift, and immediately crumpled the gift certificate into a ball with her right hand and held it in her clutched fist. "Whatever," she said. I was afraid she might punch me again.

That night, we had to throw away the pictures we developed of us standing beside the great gray slab of the bell tower, because Caroline was making stupid faces and giving me bunny ears. We had even paid extra for one-hour processing.

"Hello, Tina? What are you waiting for?"

Caroline had grown assertive. I was slight and submissive, the perfect sidekick. The week before, Caroline and I had found an old tape recorder under my grandparents' bed, and we spent the better part of the post-midnight hours roaring fake jingles for sporty Mazda Miata convertibles into the creaky reel. The innocent "Mazda MX-1, wanna go for some fun?" led to the more crass "Mazda MX-2, wanna go for a poo?" Our Mazda MX-3 jingle wasn't any better. Apparently, Caroline had brought the recording with her and stuffed it under her bed while cleaning up. I didn't want my dad finding that tape.

"Are you listening to me? Get the shit in there," Caroline demanded, aware of the fact that the word *shit* added an immediacy and forcefulness to her request, but still shaky on how to properly use it. People were right, I thought. Northerners *were* mean.

I crawled toward the open door and peered into the crypt. It smelled musty, and I couldn't see much. But before I could climb in, a hard shove pushed me deep into the dark. As I tumbled, the carpet bit hot into my palms, which slid forward in weak resistance. The door shut rapidly behind me, and I heard the sinking *clunk* of the tumbler lock latching into place. I held my stinging palms to my cheeks and emitted a single, innocent plea, as though it might have all been a mistake:

"Hello?"

Caroline laughed. In the pitch black, I finally saw what had happened. I had been duped. Sightless, I settled in to accept the inevitable taunting, but as soon as I had gotten comfortable in the dark, loud waves began to crash above my head. The squishy waterbed mattress surged thick and heavy as Caroline thrashed upon the thing, sending huge pockets of water racing through the plastic. I couldn't take it.

Panicking, I began to paw at the ground for anything useful. Heaps of clothes were no help; the stuffed animals Caroline had relegated to the darkness gave no support. Suddenly, I remembered the little trinket that Lisa bought me from the gift shop, which was still in my pocket. Blindly, I clutched onto the keychain—a small, oblong replica of the N.C. State bell tower—and thrust upward, my muscles exploding with the force of terror behind them. As Caroline jumped and rolled, water began coursing down into the cave. I started to scream.

It didn't take long for the pressure of the water to take advantage of the small hole, and soon, it was a full-fledged split. I was sitting half a foot deep by the time my dad rushed into the room and kicked down the little door.

Blinking against the light, I surveyed the scene: Caroline, in the doorway, wide-eyed; the bed, fully deflated; my dad, in shock; all of us, ankle-deep in water. Everyone stared, speechless, as I climbed out from under the bed, soaking wet. I slid the keychain back in my pocket. My stepsister started to cry. "Go to hell, Caroline," I laughed, knocking her aside with my shoulder as I walked past.

"That's it, that's enough," Lisa screamed from the hallway, her voice quivering with anger. "You're going back to Florida. I can't take it anymore." She pointed toward my open suitcase, which was sitting on the floor of the guest room, and issued a firm request. "Go pack."

"Arroooo!" I threw my head back and answered in my best wolf's howl. I swear it was snowing when I was sent home on a plane the next day.

A recent graduate of the University of North Carolina at Chapel Hill, TINA HAVER CURRIN is a copywriter for such clients as the Atlantic Coast Conference (so she finally understands what March Madness is). When she's not watching basketball, she works on her first novel, *Salesmen,* a story about growing up in downtown Raleigh.

Curtain Call

AMANDA LAMB

"MISS AMANDA, YOU KNOW YOU'RE NOT SUPPOSED to bring hairspray into the courthouse," the security officer tells me as he looks at the scan of my purse going through the x-ray machine.

"I know, but I always forget," I reply sheepishly, hoping I will not lose another 99-cent can of hairspray today. No such luck. He takes it and uses the security wand to check me after my high heels set off the metal detector.

You can grow old waiting for an elevator at the Wake County Courthouse in Raleigh. So I almost always take the stairs. As I turn the corner from the security area to the stairway, I glance at the crowd, four people deep, lining up in front of the elevator doors and wonder what they're thinking.

The courthouse stairs are scuffed from years of shoes scraping against them. The lighting is dim, and my feet echo as they click up the metal edges. The stairwell echoes with the constant sound of doors to each floor slamming shut. Some people gasp as they hold on to the metal handrail and make what could be a six-flight or more climb to the courtrooms. People whiz by distracted. They talk loudly on their cell phones, text, complain about their lawyers, about the police, about how there is no justice for them in this place. To the contrary, from my experience, the people who work here do everything they can to keep the wheels of justice grinding feverishly and with a moral compass to boot.

What I love about the cacophony is the diversity of the crowd. There are young lawyers in ill-fitting suits who awkwardly adjust their ties and mouth *hello* to me and give a slight wave as I pass. Fancy lawyers in fancy suits talk on their cell phones, far too important and far too busy to say "hello." If I'm lucky, I get a head nod. Police officers in uniform mill around, as do detectives in suits, and undercover cops with ponytails, beaded chokers, and beards. Mothers hold crying babies in their arms; young men wear chains, baseball hats, and pants that sag precariously to the floor. Scared young men in ties, flanked by their parents, prepare to plead to something they are not proud of. Women in their Sunday best stand in front of a judge and ask for mercy. Mixed in stealthily are judges who dress like everyone else, but who in a few minutes will put on black robes, climb into chairs behind an imposing bench in a courtroom, and make decisions that affect the rest of these people's lives.

I have a friend who sarcastically refers to the courthouse as "the dumpster," because of all of the struggling souls who populate it. I don't see it that way at all. I see it as a place where worlds collide — victims, suspects, law enforcement officers, and court officials. The result is an indescribable piece of theater where the roles are well-defined and often stereotypical, but never boring. It is here, in the hustle and bustle of the busiest courthouse in North Carolina, where I feel more comfortable than just about anywhere else in Raleigh. I have grown up here, both as a journalist and a woman, in these loud hallways with the scuffed walls and fluorescent lights. For eighteen years I have interviewed winners and losers, shed tears, laughed, and sighed with exasperation.

I enter each courtroom with hushed reverence. Necks of the people in the audience crane to see who is coming in. I look for action, a plea, a trial, something that I didn't know about that might be happening. Something, *anything,* that might be newsworthy. Often, I chat with the lawyers as they wait to have their cases heard. Sometimes the judge will wave me up to the front of the courtroom to speak about what is going on that day. I am always aware as I chat quietly with the judge, my back turned toward the rest of the courtroom, that the people in the audience are wondering what we are talking about. Sometimes we're talking about a case, but more often than not, we're talking about nothing—our kids, the State Fair, the weather. Judges spend so much time shrouded in the incubus of their power, sometimes they just want to have a personal conversation that has nothing to do with the cases before them.

Suddenly, my photographer, Chad, comes running in. A murder plea is happening in the next courtroom in just a few minutes. The gate between the audience and the section of the courtroom where the lawyers and judge sits makes a *whoosh* sound as Chad rushes up behind me. These are not hearings that appear on any public court calendar. You have to be in-the-know to find out when one is happening. Often, they are shoehorned in between the courthouse daily business.

"We have to go, now. I'll get the camera," he says. "We have permission to be in the courtroom. We're good to go."

Chad is my secret weapon. He's a good ol' boy from Four Oaks who has charmed just about every woman in the courthouse. As a result, *people tell him things.* He's also a character—loud, entitled, and irreverent. He can walk into a courtroom that's in session, walk right up to the bench, and speak to the judge without the usual reprimand. Like me, Chad considers the courthouse *home,* and everyone considers Chad one of the main actors in the daily drama.

I excuse myself and head across the hall to the other courtroom. This time, everyone looks up at me knowing exactly why I am there—to get video of their son, their brother, their husband, their boyfriend pleading to an unspeakable crime. On the other side of the courtroom is the family of the victim, huddled closely together just behind the prosecutors' table. At the judge's instruction, we set up the camera in the jury box facing the defendant. The lawyers from both sides speak to one another quietly as Chad sets up the microphones on the lawyers' tables and at the judge's bench. I sit in one of the ancient green leather swivel chairs in the jury box. The wooden partition in front of me is weathered and scratched, and marked with faint carvings where bored visitors have used a sharp object to permanently commemorate their day in this courtroom: *Jamie was here. Sue and Mark 4-ever.*

My reverie is interrupted as deputies bring the defendant out from the holding cell through the side door of the courtroom. He wears the traditional orange jumpsuit from the Wake County Detention Center. His ankles are shackled, so he shuffles slowly from the door to the defense table. In many ways, this is a show for the public's benefit. The lawyers have already worked out a deal, a deal they feel confident the judge will accept barring any unforeseen circumstances. The victim's family has been told what to expect, that the suspect won't get what he deserves, but he will at least be in prison for a long, long time. If they go to trial, there is no guarantee they will win. There is no guarantee he will stay locked up. The defendant's family has also been briefed. They've been told by defense attorneys that their loved one is getting a good deal, that he won't die in prison, that he'll have time to be with his family someday when he completes his sentence. The judge, too, knows that he is presiding over a plea deal. He enters, full of pomp and circumstance, carrying with him the solemn demeanor of a man who must make a grave decision when clearly one has already been made.

"All rise," the deputy says. Like a play that has been rehearsed a hundred times, the judge announces the parties have entered into a plea agreement. He asks the defendant to stand so that he may inquire whether he is entering into this agreement with full understanding that he is giving up his right to a trial by jury.

The man in the orange jumpsuit stands awkwardly in his leg irons as his attorney pulls out his chair so the defendant won't fall. As he stands, he swivels slightly to look at the audience and locks eyes with an older woman who dabs her eyes with tissue in the front row and is surely his mother. They mouth something to one another which looks like *I love you.* The attorney rests his hand on his client's shoulder and nods in the direction of the judge, a sign that now is the time for him to pay reverent attention to the man in the black robe elevated before them.

"Are you now under the influence of any drugs or alcohol that may impair your ability to enter into this plea?" the judge begins. He proceeds with a list of standard questions, and explains the defendant's right to a trial.

"Do you now plead guilty to the offenses listed in this plea agreement?"

"I do," the man responds slightly above a whisper.

"Are you in fact guilty of these charges?" the judge asks, as if he is giving the defendant one more chance to reconsider which no one ever does.

"I am," the man replies, this time a little bit louder. The older woman in the audience makes an audible cry, and then buries her face in the shoulder of a younger woman next to her, probably her daughter or daughter-in-law, who puts her hand on the woman's head and strokes her hair to comfort her. No matter how many times I see this, I am always struck that no one is ever truly prepared. There is no handbook for the family of criminals.

Attorneys for each side have an opportunity to state the facts of the case as they see them, in a clinical, sterile re-telling. While their words are powerful, the lawyers are even-toned in their delivery, as if they are reading from the phone book.

"If we were to go to trial, some of the things that we would prove beyond a reasonable doubt include the fact that the defendant did in fact in cold blood, with malice and aforethought, shoot and kill the victim on the night in question," the young prosecutor tells the judge matter-of-factly.

After prosecutors speak, it is the defense attorneys' chance to mitigate the punishment the judge is getting ready to hand down. Judges like people who take responsibility for their actions, and they especially like defendants who are remorseful.

"My client is taking responsibility for his actions," the defense attorney stresses. "He wishes that he could take them back, and that he could spare the victim's family the pain they are going through. But he can't. All he can do is move forward, spare them an emotionally draining trial, and try and be the best person he can be in prison. He has been sober since he entered the jail a year ago and would like to continue his substance abuse counseling. He is also interested in getting his GED, and being the father that he never was to his teenage son who has recently been visiting his father at the Wake County jail." The attorney goes on, building the defendant's story, until it reaches a crescendo.

I always feel slightly sorry for them, having to take so many negatives and try to make them sound positive. No matter what they say, the defense is often the same—he's had a bad life, he feels remorse, he takes responsibility, and is being transformed into a better version of himself, a person who will ultimately not be a danger to society. I believe that sometimes these things are true, and sometimes, they are not.

Just before the judge imposes the sentence, he allows the victim's family to make a "victim impact statement." They range from tearful monologues read by a parent, a child, or a spouse in front of the judge's bench, to vitriolic rants from grieving loved ones. No one has the heart to interrupt even the most emotional statements, because *this is it*—their moment to tell the defendant how they feel. Their statement doesn't change anything. The judge has usually already made up his or her mind about the sentence. But the release of their feelings in front of the defendant and the court can help them cope with their grief, anger, and sense of loss.

"Do you know what you took from us? You removed a beautiful, loving person from the world, someone with so much potential. You had no right, no right!" the sister of the victim screams, her face red and stained with tears as she points across the room at the defendant, his head hung low. He appears properly shamed by her outburst, as if these words flying at him like sharp arrows are much worse punishment than anything the judge could possibly give him.

Then it is the defendant's turn to say something to the victim's family. About half of defendants do this. Some have their attorneys read their statement. Other defendants look at the audience, usually directly at the victim's family, and make an emotional statement.

The defendant on this day rises and says, "I wish I could turn back time and go back to that night and take back my actions. I'm so sorry for what I've done. I had no right to take a life. I am especially sorry for the pain I have caused your family. I will spend the rest of my life trying to be a better person, a better man, a better father. That's all." The defendant turns away from the audience, fixes his gaze on his hands as he crumples into his seat, as if his statement has drained him of any energy to sit upright.

"Please stand," the judge says to him after giving him a brief moment to collect himself.

"Under the agreement set forth, I sentence you to twenty-five to thirty years in the North Carolina Department of Corrections," he says to the man with a booming, authoritative voice. The man stares at the judge vacantly as if none of what is being said now really matters.

"You chose this path, and now you will spend more than two decades in prison paying for your crime. You took a life, and you did it in a heinous manner, one with no regard for the victim or the victim's family. Please take this opportunity for what it is, a wake-up call, a call to become the person that you claim you want to be," the judge says sternly. I always think in this moment that if the judge had been the defendant's parent, this probably would have never happened.

And then, without fanfare, the suspect stands and turns as the deputies handcuff him and lead him toward the side door again. He pauses for a moment and turns back to his mother who has stopped crying and leans over the rail to reach out and touch him as he passes.

"Okay, we'll be at ease for a moment, take a brief break and return with the State of North Carolina versus Anderson," the judge says.

"All rise," the deputy announces. As the judge turns to leave through the back entrance of the courtroom, the side door where the defendant has just exited slams shut. A soft din fills the courtroom as people gather their belongings and shuffle out of their seats. The sound is broken only by the muffled sobs from both families—the victim's and the defendant's. The final curtain has just closed on their tragedy. In a few minutes, the curtain will re-open and a new tragedy will unfold in Raleigh's courthouse.

AMANDA LAMB is a television crime reporter for WRAL-TV and the author of seven books including *I Love You to God and Back* (an inspirational parenting book that comes in an adult and a children's version), and parenting humor books, *Girls Gone Child* and *Smotherhood*. She also writes true crime books based on the cases she covers. They include *Love Lies, Evil Next Door,* and *Deadly Dose.*

Close-ups

Backsliders

SCOTT HULER

I DID NOT GO SEE A ONE-NIGHT REUNION of the Backsliders when they recently played in downtown Raleigh, so I had to figure that a chapter in my life—and in the life of my town—had ended. I was told that Chip Robinson, the one-time frontman of the Backsliders, was by then mostly a bike messenger in New York. I had kids. I'm not sure what happened to Raleigh. But the missed reunion made me remember a time when a Backsliders show was the capital of everything Raleigh ever was, or could be.

My love affair with the Backsliders reached its apex more than a decade ago during a chance meeting on a windless summer afternoon—a Saturday, closing in on dinner time. Not too humid, but hot enough that shorts and a T-shirt were all you needed, and bordered on more than you wanted. The sun angled low, dipping the fronts of the neat mill houses across the street into shadow, but the sky remained an electric blue that seemed not to reflect light but to fairly glow. Traffic died, silence deepened. The kind of moment that makes people want to live in Raleigh.

I sat on the porch steps considering my station, and it wasn't going to wreck my day if it took two or three cigarettes to decide what to do next. Then, music.

From somewhere—south? maybe westish?—I heard the opening riff of the opening song of the Backsliders' *Throwing Rocks at the Moon*, the CD that never left my carousel that summer. Motivated, I began walking toward the sound, figuring I'd meet a neighbor with some good taste in music. Maybe we'd have a beer.

One of the delights of living in a small city, though, is that everything is kind of mixed up together. In one direction, a five-minutes' walk carries me into the city's richest neighborhood. In another, five minutes puts me among renters barely out of school. Head south—maybe westish—and I'm among warehouses and cement plants, rail yards and welding shops. Following the twang of the guitars I turned down a gravel road toward the train tracks and found Dan & Bill's Automotive (sign: *For Dan & Bill's Automotive, use 2d gate. If 2d gate is closed, so is Dan & Bill's Automotive*).

The second gate was open, and twenty or thirty people milled around in denim and cotton, smoking cigarettes, gripping sweating longnecks, and kicking up a little dust as the evening deepened. And that wasn't some Backsliders CD the neighborhood was hearing—that was the Backsliders, grinning in the dirt parking area in front of the loading dock, playing for those thirty people like they were their thirty best friends. They may have been—Chip knew a guy who owned a little company that shared space with Dan & Bill's, and it was their company picnic I had wandered into. I asked somebody if I could hang around, and I watched Robinson sing, play guitar, and dance his two-year-old son around the loading dock for the better part of two hours.

This was a new experience for me. I had had favorite groups before, but they had always been someone like Sheryl Crowe or REM or Talking Heads—people you see on TV or hear on plastic disks. People selling you something.

But not the Backsliders. The Backsliders were local. I saw them at the bar and at the bookstore, at parties and on the street. I heard when a member was sick. I knew that the oddly titled "Number 5" took its name from being the fifth song they played in their live set. They made their music from the same raw material we all shared in Raleigh, and somehow it reached me in a way that only local music can.

The Backsliders came from Raleigh, an utterly uncategorizable mixture of Southerner and transplant, of sweet tea and Jolt, of Bourbon and beer. Sleepy Southern capital with big-city pretensions? Emerging New South hotbed hamstrung by antebellum restraint? Or maybe just a good place to get a barbecue sandwich?

Hard to say. And certainly very few—whether recent transplants or fourth-generation Old Raleigh Baptists—simply take it for what it is. Everybody seems to want it to be something else: Charlotte, or Atlanta, or Austin, or Seattle, or San Jose. It can be frustrating keeping up with what a small city, growing larger, thinks it is, or thinks it might be. And the Backsliders entered my world at a time when Raleigh wasn't the only highly confused element in my life, which was skidding into the dirt with a surprising amount of momentum. My friend David surveyed the chaos for a while and then said, "There's a band you need to go see." We went to the Brewery on Hillsborough Street, a filthy, dim room with brick walls, where people stood around sweating and drinking beer from cans. The Backsliders' opening cry of *Howy'alldoing'we'reth'BackslidersfromRaleigh NorthCarolinathankyouf'rcomin'out'n'seein'us* seemed promising, but it was their advertised *Hard-Core Honky-Tonk* that caught me. First, they were loud. Second, they were good. Hard-core honky-tonk, as promised: If you were going to film the story of almost any Lucinda Williams song, these would be the guys playing in the bar. Beyond that, like Raleigh, they were hard to categorize: rock beat, yet country blues in every note; vicious guitar, yet a never-forgotten acoustic sensibility, along with the musicianship to carry everything off. The Backsliders gave that smoky, noisy bar the opportunity to be nothing but what it was: a smoky, noisy bar in Raleigh, North Carolina, on a hot summer night. Nobody there wanted to be any-where else.

David was right: The Backsliders spoke to me. I listened, and I was saved. The live EP they cut soon thereafter at the same bar—I was there, of course—put a beat in my chores for an entire season. After a while the controlled slide of my life further decompensated into a genuine wreck, and when I found myself metaphorically bloodied, dazed, and wandering around, holding the metaphorical steering wheel of my metaphorical car, there were the Backsliders, with *Throwing Rocks at the Moon*, which included the song "Crazy Wind," which I played twenty times a day and which saved my life. If the Backsliders were the band from a Lucinda Williams song, "Crazy Wind" was the song that the guy in the Eagles' "Desperado" would have sung. Since in my broken meandering I felt like I might be that guy, I liked "Crazy Wind" a lot.

The Backsliders, as I said, never left my CD carousel that year. But better than that, they never really left my life. If I went to see another band, there was Chip, at the back of the room, listening. I would bump into the lead guitarist at the supermarket, the bass player at the bar. My neighbor's friend married the rhythm guitarist. The Backsliders were just a part of my life. Not my music life—my life.

This doesn't sound like much, but if you look a little closer, it's everything. I grew up in Cleveland, Ohio, a few years too young to be part of the support for the James Gang and Joe Walsh, but I know that when I hear one of those songs there's a sound, a way they pull a string or rip a chord, that just says "Cleveland," and I'm inside. With the Backsliders I'm a little older, so I can identify more. All over *Throwing Rocks at the Moon* train whistles blow, and I remember lying in my bed during some of those awful sleepless nights and realizing: those freights I heard bumping and rumbling in the yard half a mile away, down by Dan & Bill's Automotive? Those were the same trains Chip heard when he wrote songs. And when in "Crazy Wind" Chip talked about throwing the pieces of a broken radio into a boxcar, he spoke to me of my train yard, my boxcars—the pieces of my broken things. No surprise, then, that when I needed to get rid of some objects too painful to hold onto I walked down to the yard and dumped them in a boxcar—"and let them ride to Mexico, until the truth comes drifting back on a crazy wind."

I got over it—one usually does—and the Backsliders broke up, came back, and then broke up again for good, with the exception of the very occasional reunion show. Their mixture of rock, country, and R & B still defies categorization, but somehow that just makes them more so. More what they are, and more Raleigh.

The Backsliders for a while put out a sticker, one of which is on the back of my truck now. It looks like a Heineken label, and apart from their *Hardcore honky-tonk* motto, the label bears some excellent fine print. *This ain't Nashville*, their old bumper sticker says. *This is Raleigh.* At least it was then. Since then Chip has gone to New York. Raleigh has picked up a Stanley Cup, a new convention center, and a basket more positions on national *Best place* lists but isn't the slightest bit closer to understanding itself. As for me, I'm so dug into familyville that I got a little hatchback that functions as something like a station wagon; I had to sell the old pickup truck. And that sticker wouldn't come off.

But the message, like the music, remains. If nobody else does, for a moment at least the Backsliders knew where they were. And I thank God they did. Because for a moment I believed that maybe if I followed them I'd find my way too.

SCOTT HULER moved to Raleigh in 1992 to write for the *News & Observer*. Within two years Raleigh was listed as the nation's best place for business (*Fortune*) and to live (*Money*). You may draw your own conclusions. Among the publications he has written for are the *New York Times* and *Washington Post, ESPN* magazine, and *Backpacker*. His work has been heard on such radio programs as "All Things Considered," "Marketplace," and "Splendid Table." He has written six books of nonfiction. He lives in Raleigh with his two sons and his wife, the writer June Spence.

A Force of Nature

ANDREA WEIGL

OYSTER KNIVES AND CANS of Stroh's beer in hand, four chefs sneak out the back door of Poole's Diner, the funky, acclaimed 75-seat restaurant on Raleigh's McDowell Street. It's 6:50 p.m. on a Sunday night in January, almost show time. In the dark parking lot, the chefs glow in their white jackets and aprons. They stab holes in the bottom of the cans, tilt their heads back, and down the beers in one long swig.

"Wow! That is ice cold," says Ashley Christensen, Poole's executive chef and owner.

"Brain freeze!" cries guest chef Tandy Wilson.

"Smooth!" adds guest chef Tyler Brown.

Once the ritual, borrowed from Wilson's Nashville restaurant kitchen, is complete, the chefs are ready to crank out dinner for almost fifty people who have paid $150 each for the privilege. On this weekend, Christensen and friends will raise $8,000 for the Southern Foodways Alliance (SFA), one of the handful of causes she supports.

Christensen's friends describe her as a "whirling dervish" and "a bottomless pit of energy." They talk about her passion for life, cooking, and doing good. Her two favorite causes: Southern Foodways Alliance, a nonprofit at the University of Mississippi that celebrates and documents Southern food traditions, and Raleigh's Frankie Lemmon School, which serves children with developmental disabilities.

Since 2011, Christensen has raised more than $60,000 for the SFA, as it is called by members. (A spin-off event in Nashville inspired by Ashley's efforts has raised an additional $26,500.) And she recently received an award at the Frankie Lemmon Foundation's annual gala for her innovative fundraising efforts. Christensen estimates that she and philanthropist Eliza Kraft Olander have raised more than $500,000 in the last eleven years for a variety of causes, primarily for the school and recently for SFA.

"She is a catalytic person," says John T. Edge, SFA's executive director. "She gets stuff done. She starts things and finishes things. She pulls people into the wake that follows her and does it pleasantly."

At thirty-six, Christensen is a foodie phenomenon who owns Poole's outright, having paid off her sole investor in 2010 after three years in business.

In her kitchen, Christensen, blond hair always meticulously pulled into a bun at the nape of her neck, is exacting. Before plates leave the kitchen, she wipes smears away with a damp paper towel. Waiters are expected to do the same behind her. Her obsessive tick: No kitchen towel within view is left unfolded.

In her uniform of T-shirts, slim corduroy pants, and black Birkenstock clogs, she works seventy to eighty hours a week. She is single and has a large network of friends. Sometimes she texts employees so early in the morning after a long night at the restaurant that they wonder how she manages on so little sleep.

Christensen is ambitious: After Poole's success, she has gone on to open a burger joint, a fried chicken and honey place, and an underground bar—in a 4,000-square-foot space in downtown Raleigh. Now in the works is a coffee and sandwich shop and a wood-fired oven restaurant, both downtown as well. She says the food will be "simple but with a lot of energy going into the details."

Award-winning chef John Currence, who owns the City Grocery in Oxford, Mississippi, was a guest chef at an SFA fundraiser last year and dined at Poole's the night before. He recalls the first course of pimento cheese as "this cloud of deliciousness," curled into a perfect oval on the plate and so pure that he could taste each ingredient.

"That's the mark of a great chef, when you take something as pedestrian as pimento cheese and make it transcendent," Currence says.

Christensen's national profile is rising. She has been highlighted in *Food & Wine, Bon Appetit,* and the now-defunct *Gourmet* magazine. For several years in a row, she has been a semifinalist, and this year has been named a finalist, for the James Beard Foundation Best Chef in the Southeast award—one of the highest honors for an American chef.

So much of Christensen's world involves creating community: at her restaurant, bringing people together for a meal; drinking a beer with fellow chefs before buckling down in the kitchen; rallying folks behind a cause.

Community inspired her to start a series of two-day fundraisers to benefit the SFA: The first night is the dinner at Poole's to celebrate guest chefs from out of town, the second a laidback potluck at her home that brings food industry folks together from across the Triangle.

"I really liked supporting a project that represents extended community," she says.

Her energy is a constant. At the potluck, Christensen stands in her home kitchen, with its restaurant gear, pointing out Portuguese rissoles, a breaded deep-fried pastry, that must be tasted. She dashes off to introduce someone to guest bartender Gary Crunkleton, who is making cocktails with rye, apple wine, and homemade radish bitters. Moments later, she's strolling through her patio with a garbage bag picking up trash.

The community she has created makes it seem normal to strike up a conversation with a former engineering school dean about how he ended up as a lamb farmer in Virginia or with a guest chef's girlfriend about the red Holga camera dangling around her neck.

That easy welcome is the way it's always been at Christensen's parties.

In her second year at N.C. State University, Christensen, who had a full scholarship, moved into a large old house off Hillsborough Street and started throwing dinner parties. Always with a limited budget, she cooked for four, then twelve, then thirty people.

Regardless, Christensen says, "I would challenge myself to do something I hadn't done before."

Her friend Shaun Stripling recalls: "Maybe we'd be eating on paper plates. But it was about the conversation and the music. She's really great at pulling diverse people together. Her ability to foster community is amazing."

Those parties were based on what Christensen watched her parents do back home in Kernersville. Her father was a truck driver who raised bees and grew everything from okra to asparagus in a large organic garden. Her mother was a real estate agent and an accomplished Southern cook who had learned from her grandmother. They threw large parties, serving whatever was ripe in the garden.

Those taste memories and gatherings prepared Christensen for a future as a hostess and cook, then a catering business, launched while she was in college. She asked her parents to pay for culinary school, but they couldn't afford it.

Instead, she took on restaurant jobs, first at Caffé Luna, then Humble Pie, then part-time under chef Andrea Reusing at Enoteca Vin and chef Scott Howell at Nana's.

Seth Kingsbury, who owns Pazzo! in Chapel Hill, was the chef de cuisine at Nana's when Christensen came to learn. She was working with culinary school graduates who had been trained to cut an onion precisely and how to fillet fish. But Kingsbury says that didn't deter Christensen; she asked questions and showed a thirst for learning. "She was very green," he says, "but you could tell there was something there."

By twenty-four, Christensen was executive chef at Enoteca Vin, a farm-to-table restaurant that was ahead of its time in Raleigh and closed in 2009. Eventually, she decided she wanted to pour her energy into her own business instead of working as hard as an owner but without the stake. That's why she opened Poole's Diner.

It's a decision she has never regretted. Not only has the restaurant been embraced by critics and diners, but it gives her a way to give back. She says she loves the SFA dinners and is planning several more.

At Poole's on that cold Sunday night in January, the main course of Cheerwine-braised short ribs, fried catfish, collard greens, and sorghum-glazed sweet potatoes has been served, and only dessert remains. The cakes—a play on that classic Southern combination of cornbread and buttermilk, four layers of cornbread cake with buttermilk pastry cream, covered with buttermilk frosting—sit on the restaurant's bar. They have been admired all night.

"Do we have the plates out there?" Christensen asks.

"Yes," someone replies.

"Let's do it," she says.

She, Wilson, and Brown head out to the bar. She cuts the tall cakes into sixteen slices. Brown places each slice onto a plate. Wilson sets the plates on the double-horseshoe bar for the waiters to pick up. Wilson and Christensen high-five behind the bar. Their work is done.

Then the three clink glasses of Basil Hayden's bourbon, tilt back their heads, and swig.

ANDREA WEIGL is the award-winning food writer at the *News & Observer*. Her first cookbook, *Pickles and Preserves: A Savor the South Cookbook*, will be published in 2014 from the University of North Carolina Press. The above "view" is adapted from her *News & Observer* column.

A Literary Place

BRIDGETTE A. LACY

AS A GIRL, I fell in love with Walton's Mountain, that fictional place in the foothills of the Blue Ridge Mountains where every week on the popular TV series, *The Waltons*, John-Boy found his writing voice. His stories were fueled by the simple physical beauty of the mountain, and the wisdom and love of his family, even as they struggled through the Great Depression.

When I came of age and blossomed into a writer, I longed for that kind cohesive community, one in which my talent would be nurtured and my spirit would soar no matter what the circumstances going on around me. I've lived in many places—Binghamton, New York, Indianapolis, Indiana, and Lynchburg, Virginia, and my hometown of Washington, DC.

My dream finally became real here in the City of Oaks, a place where I had no immediate family. I quickly became a part of a community not related by blood, but by the love of writing stories. They pulled me in as one of them. Never questioned my ability, just accepted my word that I was a bona fide writer, not just a journalist.

Like Walton's Mountain was for John-Boy, Raleigh became a safe place to explore my innermost feelings and let them spill out on paper for others to read, relate to, and appreciate. It was home.

My arrival in 1992 marked a change in my writing career. Hired as the first African American feature writer for the then-family-owned *News & Observer,* I made the transition from writing quick-hit deadline articles to larger, more layered stories, word pictures. I was drawn to pieces about subjects I was passionate about—authors, artists, and African American culture.

New to Raleigh, I did here what I had done earlier when I'd moved to a new city: I sought out writers. So it was natural to spend Saturday mornings browsing the aisles at Books at Quail Corners, a cozy independent bookstore located in a strip mall at the corner of Falls of the Neuse and Millbrook roads. There I met readers and local writers. It was like Walton's Mountain's general store.

Owner Nancy Olson greeted customers with a broad smile and knew everything about the local literary goings-on—who had a new novel coming out, who had just won a literary prize. Her store was quaint and intimate like a personal home library, complete with a rocking chair and an inviting large, red, damask Victorian sofa.

Writers and readers constantly found literary surprises and treasures there. Some days, Nancy and Pulitzer Prize-winning *N&O* Book Editor Michael Skube exchanged friendly banter about books and Southern literature. Customers brushed shoulders with their favorite local writers, such as novelist Angela Davis-Gardner, poet Lenard Moore, and novelist Kaye Gibbons. These authors were not just names in a book, they were real people right there in your reach.

When the store expanded and moved to Ridgewood Shopping Center, I followed. The new Quail Ridge Books drew neighbors from all over Raleigh, along with faculty and students from nearby Meredith College, North Carolina State University, and Peace College. Motorists driving by Ridgewood, the last stop inside the Beltline on Wade Avenue heading for I-40, could tell if a popular author was reading at Quail Ridge by the packed parking lot.

Over time, the store became a place to socialize as much as to shop for books and stationery. I craved the work of North Carolina writers.

I devoured Lee Smith's *Fair and Tender Ladies*; Reynolds Price's *Kate Vaiden*; and Donald Davis's *Listening for the Crack of Dawn*. Nancy always introduced me as a fellow writer to the authors who visited Quail Ridge. And they welcomed me as one of their own. They validated me as a writer even though I didn't have a book with my name on the cover yet. I was on my way.

Many of my evenings were spent at Quail Ridge Books at the readings of the very same authors I had interviewed on the phone for *News & Observer* articles. I sat mesmerized by mystery writer Walter Mosley, popular fiction author Terry McMillan, or writer Alexander McCall Smith. I wanted to know what they did. I wanted to know the secret. It was always the same. Write.

From Quail Ridge, I'd go a few doors down to shop at Wellspring Grocery, the anchor store of Ridgewood and the forerunner of Whole Foods. I filled my cart with wholesome salad greens, chicken salad, and soup to carry home to nourish my body as I worked on my stories.

On *The Waltons,* John-Boy often wrote at a desk in his bedroom, peering out at the beauty of the Blue Ridge Mountains. I wrote in my Northeast Raleigh home too, exploring ideas at my desk parked in front of a naked window that looks out to tall maples and oaks. I often sketched out stories in the soft morning light before my newspaper workday started. Many evenings, I returned to that quiet space, revising and editing, sometimes into the wee hours of the morning.

I regularly received calls from Lenard Moore, who always started the conversation the same way. "Are you writing?" He sounded like a protective brother, checking in to see if I was doing what I was supposed to be doing. Lenard and I met when I first moved to Raleigh and invited him to lunch. I could count on regularly seeing him at the main post office on New Bern Avenue with manila envelopes stuffed with manuscripts. Lenard worked downtown for the state's department of public instruction as a teacher's guide clerk, but it seemed like most of his spare time was spent crafting verse.

At least one Saturday morning every month, I drove to Southeast Raleigh to attend Lenard's Carolina African American Writers' Collective. Many black writers flocked to his 1987 ranch-style home. Some came from long distances and others from all over the Triangle. I joined the others — playwrights, poets, and fiction writers — in his family room in the basement, the literary hearth of the home.

We sat cross-legged on the carpeted floor or in folding chairs among the stacks of literary journals, poetry books, and novels as we unveiled our babies. Surrounded by the works of Harlem Renaissance writer Zora Neale Hurston, novelist Toni Morrison, poet Gwendolyn Brooks, I felt a deep sense of belonging and history.

Daylight faded into evening as we patiently waited our turn to read our newest piece of poetry or prose. We hunkered down for long hours of critiques — the supportive give-and-take of writers in community. Lenard's wife and daughter served us platters of deli meats, cheeses, condiments, and bread for sandwiches.

We entrusted each other with tender moments spun into stories and verse. Just as people of the mountain supported John-Boy's passion for writing, the collective encouraged me, pushed me to grow. I was invited to contribute to anthologies or share a spot during local readings. The members of the collective celebrated each other's successes.

But it wasn't just being part of the community at Lenard's home that created Walton's Mountain for me. It was the way Raleigh embraced writers. Nancy championed the city's writers. Her store sold 6,000 copies of Charles Frazier's debut novel, *Cold Mountain*. Kaye Gibbons talked about her writing life during radio interviews on NPR. Lee Smith reached out to writers, giving out her home telephone number.

Early on I enrolled in a fiction writing workshop at N.C. State University taught by Lee. She was the equivalent of John-Boy's Miss Hunter, giving me the nod to read my short story, "Lilly's Hunger," out loud to people who didn't know me, to see if they understood what I was trying to say. They did.

Like a den mother, Lee encouraged new writers like me. Her comments written in the margins of my short stories reassured me that I was on the right track, as I dug deeper trying to turn drafts into published stories. I would take her feedback and polish "Lilly's Hunger," until it was accepted in 1994 for the anthology, *Streetlights: Illuminating Tales of the Urban Black Experience,* which also featured the work of Terry McMillan and Bebe Moore Campbell.

The Raleigh and North Carolina writers' community was also bolstered by the presence of the North Carolina Arts Council. Located in a two-story colonial on Lane Street, the arts council promoted the state's writers and artists, awarding fellowships every other year, giving them time to create new work.

The arts council was housed in a 1917 brick home with hardwood floors. Literature Director Debbie McGill worked in a sunny corner office on the first floor of the quaint home. Debbie made writers feel special, diligently listening to us plot our careers and offering sound advice and resources. Sometimes, we walked down the one-way street, to the locally owned Side Street Restaurant for a sandwich and a sweet tea. As we passed the governor's mansion across the street from the arts council, I anticipated a meal as special as the ones served there.

I followed Debbie's advice when I spilled out my heart in my arts council application narrative and sent what I considered the best sample of my work. I spoke of how "I had the courage to express myself in writing, in a way I never could verbally . . . I imagined a better life for myself through writing." I was rewarded with a 1994 North Carolina Arts Council fellowship to travel to LaNapoule, France. That trip inspired me to work part-time at the newspaper and dedicate more time to the writing of my choosing.

I was growing as a nonfiction writer as well, not just reporting on other people's lives but publishing first-person pieces about the things I knew best. I penned a first-person piece on surviving a brain tumor and another on the joy of bath nights at my grandparents' Virginia home. I was also expanding my range beyond the confines of print, and began to record first-person essays for WUNC Radio. Both in print and on the radio, I revealed those small intimate details of my life that echoed something familiar to readers and listeners.

I started building an audience. Readers recognized my byline, my unique voice. Once, I was waiting for a doctor's appointment, and when the nurse called me in, a reader in the waiting room complimented my work as soon as she heard my name. Another time, a teller praised my work as I cashed checks at the bank's drive-through. Readers sent letters thanking me for capturing a particular experience or person.

Their kind words feed my soul. Like John-Boy, I am humbled that they have chosen me to say grace.

BRIDGETTE A. LACY draws on life-defining moments to produce her prose and fiction. She writes about everything from her challenge of being the first person in her family to graduate from high school and college, to her battle with a brain tumor. She was the recipient of a 1994 North Carolina Arts Fellowship. Her short story, "Lilly's Hunger," was published in *Streetlights: Illuminating Tales of the Urban Black Experience.* Her work has appeared in the *Washington Post, Newsweek,* and *Southern Living.*

Where the Beauty Lies

LIZA ROBERTS

YOU MIGHT NOT KNOW IT, but you've probably seen Thomas Sayre's art.

It's big, it's bold, and it's public. In Raleigh, his three gigantic earthen ellipses spool across a field at the North Carolina Museum of Art. His comet-inspired, curvilinear patio at Broughton High School is packed with kids. His undulating oak tree shimmers on the exterior of the Raleigh Convention Center, and his wall clad with 1.1 million marbles at Marbles Kids Museum glows in the night.

Other cities in other states have the Sayre touch as well: Nashville's Public Square is dominated by his towering glass human figure; at the University of Colorado Denver's medical school campus, a quarter-mile promenade is dedicated to his orbs. Sayre's works also define public spaces in cities like Oklahoma City, Clearwater, Florida, and Calgary, Alberta.

The maker of this art that grabs your attention and makes you look, even if you're whizzing past by car or on foot, is a man of human dimensions and modest demeanor. "I work hard, which is what I do," he says. "I work really hard." Sayre's work is both conceptual and physical, requiring the metaphoric skills of a poet, the grit of a backhoe driver, and the ingenuity of an inventor. He learned to make his earthcasts — concrete sculptures cast in freshly dug earth that incorporate the soil—by experimenting repeatedly in a friend's field. He got the public-art-spooked City of Raleigh to approve his convention center shimmer wall in part by referring to it, in plans, as a "louver," since, in fact, it is just that: Behind its fluttering, reflective petals lie the building's giant vents.

"I like to know when I'm making art, and when I'm being entrepreneurial," Sayre says, but he often combines the two successfully. "My wife has a theory that I have a really large *corpus callosum"*—that fibrous tissue that connects left and right sides of the brain.

Sayre's base of operations, the art and architecture firm Clearscapes, which he founded with architect Steve Schuster, is a physical manifestation of just that. Tucked in former warehouse space downtown, where it sprawls, the outfit makes both buildings and art, and each side helps the other. Clearscapes' hushed, tidy, high-ceilinged offices with rolling-ladder bookcases give way to the noise and mess of chainsaws, steel, and welding next door on one side, and Sayre's home on the other, where he lives with his wife, Joan-Ellen Deck, and their teenage daughter. An older daughter is at University of North Carolina at Chapel Hill.

Now sixty-one, Sayre moved to this spot twenty-two years ago. "Coming from fifty acres in Rutherford County, this was like a big city," he says. "And it's become much more of a big city since then."

His work has become bigger as well, both in size and in impact. One reflection of that is the North Carolina Award he received in 2012 from the North Carolina Department of Cultural Resources. It is known as one of the highest civilian honors bestowed by the state.

"I was sort of a hippie, a hippie that had some ambition, I guess," Sayre says of his younger self. A Morehead Scholar at UNC-Chapel Hill, Sayre spent his childhood in the rarified surroundings of Washington National Cathedral, where his father served as dean. The cathedral was under construction when the Sayre family arrived in 1950, and was completed under his father's direction. Sayre befriended the carvers and workers whose ancient skills finished the majestic space around them.

"From the age of six or eight, I realized that three-dimensional space, and what expresses it—walls, windows, art—is capable of transmitting deep human meaning and emotion. I had greatest respect for the guys who carved, made stained glass, and mixed the mortar." The pings and clinks of their hammers and tools punctuated the Sayre family's daily life.

It was an enriching place in other ways, too. Guests at the cathedral dinner table could include a presidential candidate one evening and a homeless person the next. "I learned the bell curve of distribution of good folk and not good folk is the same on the street as it is in the U.S. Congress," Sayre says. When Martin Luther King Jr. preached at the cathedral and had "the traditional Sunday dinner preceded by sherry" at the Sayre house afterward, "I regarded him as just another human being I could connect to." Four nights later, King was dead. Sayre sat on top of the cathedral to see the fire of riots across Rock Creek Park.

If home provided a rare education, actual school was a mess. Dyslexic in an era when the condition was little understood, Sayre says he was "an academic disaster" in his early school years. But he adapted, through unfashionable methods like rote memorization, as well as practical ones like listening to Shakespeare's plays on 78 rpm records instead of reading them.

He also found success in art, which buoyed him. Part-time work with a welder in high school taught him enough that he could create figures in the style of Giacometti, which he sold. Hard work meant that his grades were eventually good enough to get him that Morehead Scholarship.

These days, Sayre's inspirations come from all kinds of places. The marble-dazzled wall at Marbles (which was then the museum Exploris) was inspired by an old-fashioned Lite-Brite toy he found at a friend's house. When the museum merged and grew, it didn't have to look far for its new name.

When the University of Colorado Denver sought a monumental piece of art for a quarter-mile stretch between campuses, the Raleigh artist created two 14-foot-diameter spheres (one a grid of steel, one of earth-cast concrete) on either end of a series of "outdoor rooms." Sayre was inspired by the idea that science, represented by the steel orb, connects to life, represented by the earthcast orb, through a series of conversations and negotiations that take place between people and ideas. The inspiration is made clear in the piece's title, one close to Sayre's heart: *Corpus Callosum.*

The question of balance—between science and life, between intent and serendipity, between art and nature—intrigues him. In his earthcasts, "There is always a place where the earth ends and the manmade concrete begins." That line of demarcation, "the balance between nature-made and human-made," fascinates him.

"The earth took hundreds of thousands of years to build," he says, "and we come along with diesel-powered human tools and drawing ability and say, 'I'm gonna make a sphere.' But the sphere you get is not that sphere that you plan, it is this sphere that emerges."

To Sayre, that's where the beauty lies. "That's more like life itself, as I know life to be."

As a result, the sphere that emerges—or the towering, mystical ellipses that roll across the field at the North Carolina Museum of Art—says as much about the place that grew it as it does about the artist himself. "I know artists who think they can control everything," Sayre says. "I don't want to work that way. The older I get, the more faith I have to take risks."

LIZA ROBERTS is the editor and general manager of *Walter,* a Raleigh city magazine. She is the author of *Europe's A-List.*

Views from Before

The Third House

ROB CHRISTENSEN

IN MOST STATE CAPITALS, there is one hotel that is the state's political epicenter—the place where deals are cut, satchels of campaign money are exchanged, and gossip is traded over bourbon.

In North Carolina, that place was the Sir Walter Hotel, a ten-story brick building located at 400 Fayetteville Street.

Because the state's pre-Civil War–era capitol is so small, state legislators needed a place to meet, meet with lobbyists, constituents, and just hold court. So much state business was conducted at the Sir Walter that it was nicknamed "The Third House" of the general assembly.

"The saying is that there were more bills passed at the Sir Walter than in the Capitol," Arthur Buddenhagen, manager of the Sir Walter from 1947 to 1967, once told me. "There is a lot of truth to that."

North Carolina's first political hotel was the Yarborough House, which was built in 1852 and burned down in 1928. The Sir Walter, built in 1924, catered to rich Northerners traveling by train to Florida and to the convention trade. It was regarded as the city's most elegant hotel, with dinner served by white-gloved black waiters.

After World War II, the tourist trade declined, but it became a convention and social center. The Sir Walter was where young women from the state's leading families stayed every fall to be presented at the North Carolina Debutante Ball. The hotel was the home of socially prominent clubs such as the City Club, the Sphinx Club, and the Sir Walter Cabinet.

By 1925, it was estimated that 80 percent of the legislature stayed at the Sir Walter when it was in session.

Several state officials, such as longtime State Treasurer Edwin Gill, lived there full-time in an apartment. Gill wrote an unpublished novel called *The Night Clerk,* which was set in a hotel very much like the Sir Walter. In the novel, Gill recalls the smell of stale tobacco smoke, giving "a masculine scent to the lobby."

The actual hotel was filled with "legislators and poker players, the prostitutes who slip in despite vigilance, the salesmen, the highway contractors, the lawyers, the members of boards and commissions, the delegations, the conventions, the Young Democrats and the lady Democrats," wrote newspaperman Jonathan Daniels in 1941.

With so many men in Raleigh separated from their wives, there were the predictable hijinks. Robert I. Lee, the Sir Walter manager from 1929 to 1934, remembers the time two legislators were plying a young woman with liquor when she passed out. The men panicked, with one inebriated lawmaker running pantless down the hallway yelling that there was a dead woman in his room. The lawmaker later regained his equilibrium and went back and revived the woman.

Because of Raleigh's Southern Baptist culture, there was no political saloon in the state capital. But that didn't mean there wasn't plenty of drinking in the Sir Walter Hotel. Much of it was free booze supplied by the liquor lobby.

Tipped off by a local Baptist minister, the Rev. Gerald C. Primm, the *News & Observer* in May 1957 photographed liquor lobbyists unloading twenty-seven gallons of liquor at the rear of the Sir Walter. Every Monday morning, with the help of a bellboy, a local liquor salesman delivered as many as nine cases of liquor. The booze went to Room 215, which was permanently rented by the liquor lobby, where the bottles were distributed to lawmakers' rooms in brown paper bags.

U.S. Senator Sam Ervin Jr. once called it "the most politically saturated inn in America," and it was the preferred location of political campaigns.

A canvass in December 1971 found the following. On the eighth floor was the headquarters of Roy Sowers, a candidate for lieutenant governor. On the seventh floor was the campaign office of Attorney General Robert Morgan, who was then thinking of running for governor. On the sixth floor was the headquarters of Allen Barbee, a candidate for lieutenant governor. On the fifth floor was the office of Lieutenant Governor Pat Taylor, a candidate for governor. On the fourth floor was the office of Hector McGeachy, a state senator looking at running for attorney general. On the third floor was the headquarters for Hargrove "Skipper" Bowles, a Democratic candidate for governor. The state Democratic headquarters was on the mezzanine. And Room 101 was the state headquarters for presidential candidate Ed Muskie, the senator from Maine.

All were Democrats, and none gained the offices they were seeking that year. (Morgan bypassed the governor's race and was re-elected attorney general.)

In 1963, the Sir Walter Hotel became the target of civil rights demonstrators, and lawmakers, returning from a day at the legislature, often had to make their way through singing, clapping demonstrators in the lobby. The sit-ins helped provoke a backlash that resulted in legislative passage that year of the Speaker Ban Law, which prohibited communists from speaking on state-supported campuses. Many rural lawmakers equated the civil rights movement with communism—part of an incomprehensible plot to destroy the Southern way of life.

The decline of the Sir Walter began when the North Carolina State Legislative Building was opened in 1963, providing office and committee room space for lawmakers. It was also a block farther away from the legislature than the capitol. The Sir Walter was also hurt by the decline of Raleigh's downtown.

Soon lawmakers were heading for newer hotels on Hillsborough Street and later still, as the length of sessions grew, to apartments.

The state Democratic Party moved out of the Sir Walter Hotel in 1975. Three years later, the old hotel was turned into apartments for the elderly, and it remains so today.

ROB CHRISTENSEN, who moved to Raleigh in 1973, has been writing about North Carolina politics as a reporter and columnist for the *News & Observer* for nearly forty years. He has contributed to three books and is the author of *The Paradox of Tar Heel Politics.*

Harking Back to Hargett Street

ELEANORA E. TATE

JOHN BERENDT'S *Midnight in the Garden of Good and Evil* was the only book I'd heard of that led to a walking tour, until my own *Celeste's Harlem Renaissance* "Walking Tour" of Raleigh came along.

Berendt's nonfiction book takes place in the 1980s in Savannah, Georgia, and recounts a scandalous murder there. *Celeste's Harlem Renaissance,* my eleventh book, takes place in Raleigh and in Harlem in 1921, and is historical fiction.

I'm still amazed at how the *Celeste* tour came about. When it was published in early April 2007, *Celeste's Harlem Renaissance* caught the attention of the *News & Observer* Lifestyles editor Weta Ray Clark and writer Bridgette Lacy. At about the same time, Hargett Street and the surrounding downtown Raleigh were attracting media and developers' attentions.

Clark and Lacy thought a fact-filled walking tour about some of the same Raleigh businesses and buildings mentioned in *Celeste's Harlem Renaissance,* and which also happened to have been closed up, torn down, or otherwise changed, would be interesting.

Though thrilled with the idea, I'd spent the previous four years conducting meticulous research and churning out nearly three hundred pages to produce *Celeste*. I'd also been teaching children's literature at North Carolina Central University and working with creative writing students as an Institute of Children's Literature instructor. My brain couldn't organize anything as complicated as a tour.

But when Wanda Cox-Bailey, branch manager of the Richard B. Harrison Library on New Bern Avenue, assured me that she and librarian Thomas Hancock, who also owned Capital City Tours, would handle the logistics, I agreed. After all, they were historians with long memories, and they could walk, talk, and think at the same time—skills that I had temporarily misplaced.

My *Celeste's Harlem Renaissance* book launch was held on my birthday in April at the Richard B. Harrison Library. At about the same time the *N&O* printed a *huge* story about the book, Hargett Street, and me, and even created a mostly accurate map that displayed the tour route.

Then came the tour. On April 28, 2007, about sixty men, women, children, and I stood on East Hargett Street while Mr. Hancock and Mrs. Bailey discussed African American–owned businesses that once flourished there. My late husband, Zack E. Hamlett III, and his friend, the late Lawrence Wilson, trotted about, taking photos, which I still cherish.

In *Celeste's Harlem Renaissance* I had tried to capture a portion of the historical life, a sense of place (my favorite literary element), and the sensibilities of Black Raleigh and Black Harlem as experienced through the eyes of my fictional narrator, Celeste Lassiter Massey. I was not around in 1921, of course, so I faced a considerable challenge to make Celeste's story in the City of Oaks and in the Big Apple resonate with readers. Guess I did. *Celeste's Harlem Renaissance* garnered the North Carolina Chapter of the American Association of University Women's 2007 Juvenile Literature Award and became a 2008 International Reading Association Teacher's Choice winner.

Thirteen-year-old Celeste lives with her ailing World War I–veteran father Taylor Massey and her picky, poking, prying, and permanently peeved spinster aunt, Society Massey. At its heart, *Celeste* explores the world of a precocious African American teen living in rigid segregation, confronted with life-changing choices that involve not only her own destiny but also that of her family.

In my book Celeste lives on Swain Street (an actual street) near downtown Raleigh. She often visits the graves of her mother, baby brother, and grandparents in Raleigh City Cemetery, which was established in 1798 on 7.68 acres at Hargett and East streets and New Bern Avenue. It's the oldest public burial ground in town, and many of Raleigh's founding fathers—military, civic, business, political, and other leaders—lie there. A portion of the cemetery was set aside early on for enslaved and free African Americans and the poor.

Two African American dignitaries buried there are Dr. Anna Julia Cooper (born in 1858) and her husband, the Rev. George Cooper, an educator and a Saint Augustine's College (now University) chaplain. Dr. Anna Cooper was an internationally known educator, author, poet, and an early advocate of equal rights for African Americans and women. She was a graduate of Saint Augustine's, where she also taught. She died in 1964. In 2009, a U.S. postage stamp was released in her honor.

West on Hargett Street, near the current central bus terminal location, was the site of the Lightner Arcade and office building, built by the influential businessman Calvin Lightner back in the day. The arcade featured a hotel and a variety of Negro businesses, including beauty salons, dentists, lawyers, barbershops, a shoeshine shop, and educator Charles N. Hunter's newspaper, the *Raleigh Independent*.

The Lightner was a loose prototype for my book's Stackhouse Hotel, where Celeste works with her father in its gift shop and apothecary. Since "Stackhouse" is a popular Southern name, I also chose it for the last name of my main character, Raisin, in my 1987 book, *The Secret of Gumbo Grove* (set in South Carolina).

Celeste's Aunt Valentina Chavis, who Celeste lives with during her stint in Harlem, stays at the Stackhouse Hotel after she returns to perform at the North Carolina Negro Great State Fair held in Raleigh each fall.

This very real fair was created after the Civil War by the North Carolina Industrial Commission, a Negro professional organization. The fair highlighted the accomplishments of North Carolina African Americans in agriculture, the arts and literary work, education, and business—or "farm, field, home, and health," as Celeste's teacher, Mrs. Bracy, tells her students when they board a bus to go see the fair's parade in downtown Raleigh. The fair annually drew thousands of visitors, participants, and politicians from around the South and East, as well as prominent Negroes like Frederick Douglass and Booker T. Washington. The fair closed after 1930. (I'm currently working on a book about this fair.)

158

Back to the tour. Mr. Hancock and Mrs. Bailey periodically pointed to buildings or empty lots where businesses like the Royal Theater used to be. In *Celeste's Harlem Renaissance*, this is the area near the Lightner office building. Celeste, her friends, and other Negro patrons watch silent movies and "talkies" at the Royal.

At our next stop, we looked at a real building. Known as the oldest African American–owned pharmacy in the country, Hamlin Drug at 126 East Hargett Street is still in business.

Begun in 1904 as People's Drug Store, it was renamed Hamlin Drug in 1907. At one time it was said to have been located on the first floor of the Lightner Arcade, according to a Raleigh convention brochure I found. Hamlin's is one of the best examples of Raleigh's surviving downtown Negro businesses from the 1920s.

Although we didn't walk to it, the Dr. M.T. Pope House still sits at 511 South Wilmington Street. Its owner was Manassas Pope, a well-known Negro medical doctor, surgeon, and politician who fought hard for equal rights in the midst of rabid segregation. His office was at 13 East Hargett Street.

In my book, Celeste and her father are patients of Dr. Pope, who determines that Celeste's father has tuberculosis—known in those days as consumption—and must enter Coopers Colored Sanitarium outside of Oxford for a spell. Mr. Massey's hospitalization forces Celeste to spend the spring and summer in Harlem with her once-rich-but-now-poor, floor-and-wall-scrubbing, flighty actress aunt, Valentina Chavis, a former Raleighite.

Speaking of Harlem: In order for Celeste to enter the glitter and grime of Harlem at the beginning of its artistic renaissance, I immersed myself as best as I could into New York life of 1921, from Lenox Avenue to Broadway, from my fictional Cafe Noir Le Grande to the Statue of Liberty, from Pig Foot Mary to Madame C.J. Walker, and from Duke Ellington and James Weldon Johnson to Eubie Blake, Noble Sissle, and their groundbreaking musical, *Shuffle Along.*

The modern, culturally sophisticated Raleigh of the 1920s that I wrote about featured powerful Negro men's and women's civic, social, literary, and benevolent associations, men's and women's clubs, Masonic lodges, and other fraternal organizations. Many men and women held prestigious jobs in education, like those in Celeste's school and at Shaw, Saint Augustine's, and the Berry O'Kelly School, among others. A few had good jobs in state government.

Young men and women sought to become medical, dental, law, and women's haircare professionals, and restaurant owners. Then as now, men's barbershops were gathering places. Some men, like Celeste's neighbor, Mr. Smithfield, held coveted jobs as railroad porters. Mrs. Smithfield, Celeste's reliable friend, was a cook in the governor's mansion. Although Aunt Society is a terrible seamstress, numerous Raleigh men and women were excellent clothiers and milliners. Many African Americans were maids, butlers, and chauffeurs in wealthy white and Negro homes.

Still, North Carolina's overall lack of sanitary procedures caused terrible health hazards for all residents, regardless of ethnicity. Parasitic diseases from outhouses and open sewers commingling with water supplies were deadly. Lack of vaccines for flu, tuberculosis, polio, and other diseases resulted in hundreds of deaths. Heart attacks, strokes (which Aunt Society suffers while Celeste is away), pneumonia, the common cold, and other illnesses regularly felled residents.

Many Negroes lived in deep poverty. Formerly enslaved persons, the elderly, and indigent Negroes languished on poor farms and in mental institutions, were incarcerated, rightly or wrongly, and, tragically, too often were lynched.

Raleigh's Negro churches administered to those sick in body as well as in spirit. Celeste and her father belong to St. Paul AME Church on Edenton Street, one of the oldest, largest, and most powerful African Methodist Episcopal churches in the state. When Aunt Society isn't feuding with the pastor, she attends one or another of the plentiful Baptist Negro churches. Missionary societies in most, if not all, Negro churches sought to provide food, shelter, and overall assistance to anyone in need, young and old.

While in Harlem, Celeste witnesses her own "renaissance," and just in time, because she must abruptly go back home to nurse cranky Aunt Society who nobody else wants to deal with. Most important, Celeste prays that she can get back into grade school, graduate, and eventually fulfill her dream to become a medical doctor. Aunt Society has always maintained that Celeste should attend Saint Agnes Hospital and Training School for Nurses on the Saint Augustine's campus — but only to learn how to empty bedpans.

Had I chosen an earlier period in which to place my young narrator, I could have allowed her to assume that she'd attend Shaw University's medical school before it ceased operations. That would have been too easy an obstacle for Celeste to overcome.

Lest anyone think that the real Raleigh in 1921 was completely cosmopolitan, outhouses still existed, and some residents raised chickens, guinea hens, ducks, mules, horses, and probably a goat or pig or two. Ox carts and horse wagons were common. In my book such livestock poops all over the place, especially in Celeste's backyard under the clothesline.

When Aunt Society's frail health worsens, in desperation Celeste decides to scrub floors and clean houses in the evenings, stay with her aunt at night, and go to school during the day. It seems that the girl's efforts to even get into eighth grade—let alone look to the year when she can eventually go to medical school—will fail.

Well, what happens next? Read *Celeste's Harlem Renaissance* to find out. And take a walk down Hargett Street, too.

ELEANORA E. TATE is the author of eleven children's and young adult books. Her books have garnered numerous awards, including the Parents Choice Awards, ABA Pick of the Lists, Notable Children's Trade Books, and a Bankstreet Child Study Book Committee Children's Book of the Year. Her book, *Just an Overnight Guest,* was adapted into an award-winning television film. She is an instructor at the Institute of Children's Literature and on the faculty of Hamline University.

Raleigh Jazz Festival, 1986

LENARD D. MOORE

On Fayetteville Street Mall
a lean man bobs his head.
His sax shines — polished
copper in a sunbeam,
rhythm, a splendid rising
echoing against concrete.

The trumpeter inches
across the homemade platform;
his angled jaw swerves
and slacks.
His notes — perfect
geometry for dancing.

People snap their fingers;
they are bassline
vibrating autumn.
Pigeons peck peanuts,
drum beaks
on the sidewalk.

The musicians blast into sky,
ripple red leaves loose
from a stand of trees,
glow in the sunset,
play vamps
as earthlings will do.

LENARD D. MOORE is the author of *A Temple Looming* and *Forever Home,* among other books. He is the recipient of many awards, including the Raleigh Medal of the Arts, the Sam Ragan Fine Arts Award, the Indies Arts Award, and three-time recipient of the Haiku Museum of Tokyo Award. He is founder and executive director of the legendary Carolina African American Writers' Collective and is a Cave Canem graduate fellow. A North Carolina native, he is an associate professor of English at Mount Olive College.

Dining at Balentine's

DANA WYNNE LINDQUIST

MY FATHER'S FATHER, Robert W. Wynne Jr., was not an easy man to know. In fact, he confounded me — and others — with his mix of tender-heartedness, sternness, and affability. I saw him tear up and pull out his white handkerchief to dab the corners of his eyes on more occasions than I can count. Occasions when no one else was crying. It is hard to imagine how he got through each day of his career as a funeral director who witnessed, dignified, and softened the grief of others as best he could. But at Raleigh's Brown-Wynne Funeral Home and at his own home in the Budleigh neighborhood, he ran a tight ship. A light left on or off, a sofa cushion not plumped, a phone call not responded to promptly — all could elicit a sharp word. And yet he loved to tell and to hear a good joke, share a stiff drink with a golfing buddy, write a corny poem for each family occasion, enjoy slow-cooked vegetables at Balentine's Cafeteria.

In the sixteen years since "Ganddaddy" died, I have wondered if some of his sharpness didn't come from seeing, funeral after funeral, all the ways lives can end abruptly, unjustly. He knew better than most how little control each of us has. So he cared about managing the details. In every particular, he was determined to convey his respect for the families he served in his funeral business. Coming of age during the Depression, he learned to tend to his belongings, to tend to his friends, and to tend to his savings. And he appreciated people who did likewise. Which is why the one thing that always made sense to me about my grandfather was his love for Balentine's Cafeteria, an old Raleigh institution that for nearly forty years served as a gathering place for many capital city families.

Located near the corner of Oberlin Road and Clark Avenue, Balentine's was an anchor in Cameron Village, Willie York's ambitious mixed-use development that opened in 1949. When the plan for Cameron Village was fully realized, it boasted 112 offices, 65 stores, 566 apartment units, and 100 private homes. In 1960, the cafeteria moved to "the Village" from its Fayetteville Street location, where it had been since 1950. Founder "Red" Balentine, who had previously owned and run the Green Grill on Salisbury Street and the Cardinal Room beneath his Fayetteville Street cafeteria, had little dining competition when he moved to Cameron Village. "The other establishments were delis and soda shops," recalls Red's son John, who joined the business in 1961 and took over the helm in 1974.

The cafeteria occupied a building at 410 Oberlin Road that was designed by modernist architect Leif Valand. It exemplified the Prairie School of architecture with its flat roof and its strong horizontal lines interrupted by a dramatic vertical column of glass that revealed the staircase. Textured brick and river rock formed the exterior. Because the building was, oddly, oriented perpendicular to the street, the only way to appreciate its geometry was to stand in the expansive parking lot that abutted it.

From the street, a stone wall displayed in elegant cursive letters *Balentine's* and announced *The Confederate House*, the Balentine family's below-ground, full-service restaurant that eventually became a banquet facility for hosting civic clubs and catering events. My grandfather would have missed the sad irony of the Confederate House located on a street named for the abolitionist-led Oberlin College and home to nearby Oberlin Village, one of Raleigh's first freedmen communities.

165

In fact, I'm pretty sure that, though Ganddaddy loved Raleigh history, none of the striking facts of the building much mattered to him. As far as he was concerned, 410 Oberlin wasn't "flashy"—his descriptor for so many things he hated.

Balentine's and its parking lot functioned a bit like a town square for my grandfather and his contemporaries. You could show up there any week-night and, from the moment you stepped out of your car, find neighbors and acquaintances to chat with. "We opened at four o'clock," recalls John Balentine, a contemporary of my father and a high school classmate of my aunt. "And there was a crowd that gathered in the lobby *before* four o'clock so they'd be there when the line opened. It didn't make any sense to me at the time. But now that I'm up in years, it does. Those regulars knew they could socialize and talk and get their food before the crowds arrived. They had their positions, first in line, second in line, et cetera. Folks got a little bent out of shape if someone took their position. Honestly, I thought it was kind of funny, and I wondered about old people. But here I am now myself. I realize we really provided something for them."

"Once your grandmother died," Balentine tells me, "Mr. Wynne ate with us almost every weekday evening. People loved to see him. He was a real Southern gentleman, and he loved people."

Balentine's wasn't just for senior citizens. To Raleigh families with multiple generations in close proximity, meeting at Balentine's was a com-fortable, economical way to catch up midweek—without anyone having to cook for the whole clan. Matriarchs and patriarchs could show off their brood to their bridge club or golfing friends. On a typical evening, the wait might be twenty or thirty people deep. But no one cared. The line moved quickly enough. Parents pushed toddlers in wheeled highchairs, while grandparents assisted young grandkids with their food selection or que-ried teens about their school day. And progressing through the line created a chance for reconnecting with other families: meeting the newest baby, getting the report on someone who'd been sick, hearing about the young adult away at college.

Steam rose from the chicken potpie, the fried flounder, the macaroni and cheese, the collard greens. A buxom lady, hairnet pulled over a tightly coiffed bun, greeted each customer with a patient smile and a Southern "Can I hep you?" Each server moved you along briskly. Always, there were congealed salads beautifully displayed over crushed ice, pies and cakes, sweet tea and chocolate milk.

Balentine's was family. The staff took care of you, assisted you with your tray and in finding you a table, often near friends or relatives—all of whom they knew. In fact, Balentine's was literally family: For decades, my grandfather's nephew Milton Hayes helped manage the smooth operation.

Once you'd been seated, socializing in the dining room was as important as eating. Folks politely excused themselves from their tables to speak to someone across the room. Both my grandfather and father, whose family first came to Raleigh in the early 1800s, seemed to know everyone. Balentine's was one of the few places where I heard my father called "Bobby" by the ladies who had known him since he was a little boy.

It strikes me now that the dignified but relaxed environment the Balentine family created made dining out a friendly concept to my grandfather's generation. When Balentine's developed its following, Raleigh had no chain restaurants, and dining out options were few and mostly formal— reserved for anniversaries and big birthdays. The cafeteria was less than two and half miles from Ganddaddy's back door and closer still to where his childhood home once stood on Hillsborough Street, across from the NCSU bell tower. So it's no surprise that Balentine's felt familiar.

For Ganddaddy's eightieth birthday, my parents honored his no-fuss preference with a midday brunch at the Confederate House, which was already decorated for the Christmas holidays—a practicality our frugal patriarch loved. He joked that all his friends would likely already have plans to come to Balentine's that day anyway, making it less of a to-do in his mind than if they had gone out of their way to celebrate his life.

With my one-year-old daughter on my hip, surrounded by my siblings and cousins, our spouses and children, I looked around the room that day at the familiar faces of my childhood. Since I had returned with my husband to Raleigh in 1991, I'd dined with many of them at Balentine's.

My dad surprised his father with a video that pieced together old black and white photos of his eighty years in Raleigh: Ganddaddy and his sister Lula on a horse on Hillsborough Street, graduation in the first senior class at Broughton High School, undergraduate shenanigans at NCSU, my grandparents' wedding in Boylan Heights, welcoming my infant father home from the old Rex Hospital. The images reminded me of how intricately my grandfather's history, and that of three generations before him, was interwoven with the history of the city. I was not surprised to look over at Ganddaddy and find him dabbing his eyes with his handkerchief.

In the fall of 2011, driving down Oberlin Road, I came upon the demolition of the old Balentine's building. I had to pull the car over and sit there a while, watching. The restaurant had closed its doors in 1999, but 410 Oberlin Road would always be Balentine's to me. Somehow, I'd missed the news that this piece of history was destined for the wrecking ball. Turns out, not many people appreciate the modernist designs constructed in the capital city during the 1950s and 1960s. Some experts say that the Balentine's building was Raleigh's last remaining example of the Prairie School movement. By mid-2013, a multi-story, mixed-use complex will span the corner of Oberlin and Clark. In form and style, it will be a far cry from the simpler aesthetics of its predecessor. And the sophisticated eateries that will surely open there will be a far cry from the à la carte homeyness of Balentine's.

DANA WYNNE LINDQUIST has written about North Carolina homes, art, architecture, and authors for various publications, including the former *NC Home* magazine and *Duke Magazine*. She holds an A.B. from Duke University and an M.A. in Creative Writing/ English from North Carolina State University. She has taught English at Peace College (now William Peace University), North Carolina State University, and Ravenscroft School. She and her family live in North Raleigh, just a few miles from the farm where her great-great-great-grandfather, Robert Wynne, was born in 1813.

Gateway to the Past

KELLY STARLING LYONS

WHEN I CAME TO RALEIGH, I didn't know what to expect. Culturally rich and family-focused, it felt familiar and foreign at the same time. The friendliness reminded me of my Pittsburgh hometown. But though I met many transplants like me from the North, Raleigh was unmistakably Southern. Tea was served sweet. A house of worship was a staple. And elders wanted to know who your people were. They asked, not to be nosy but to affirm that you were part of a legacy. You came from somebody.

As I got to know my new city and the people who called it home, I felt the pull of history. Being here—where enslaved African Americans toiled and prayed for freedom, where foot soldiers of the civil rights movement stood up for equality and justice, where African Americans created thriving businesses and art—pieces of the past connected with my soul in a deep and lasting way. The stories my grandparents had told and events I read about in history books came to life as I explored the city and put down roots. Raleigh was a gateway.

After we married, my husband and I became members of Saint Paul AME on Edenton Street. Church history says it's the oldest black church in Wake County. In that sacred space, I sang hymns and spirituals I remembered from childhood. As the congregation's chorus of voices merged into one, the music filled me up just like it had when I was young. But I felt something else when I sang the words, too. Laced between the lyrics was the knowledge that some of these songs were sung during slavery. Some of the songs were sung through the joys of emancipation and the realities of Reconstruction. These songs were a testament to folks whose belief in God carried them through unimaginable struggles and delivered them to a new life. I could feel their faith and love.

Everywhere I looked, I found bridges to yesterday. Family friends lived near Chavis Park, named for John Chavis, a free African American teacher and minister who taught black and white children in Raleigh in the 1800s. One of my friends told me about how families would flock to the park to ride the beautiful carousel and splash in a pool that attracted visitors from other states.

Driving to Krispy Kreme took me past Peace College. The main building, I learned, had been a district headquarters for the Freedmen's Bureau where freedmen and -women could receive help with getting an education and securing jobs. A visit to Shaw University revealed that the Student Nonviolent Coordinating Committee (SNCC), one of the vital organizations of the civil rights movement, was founded there. I marveled at the historical treasures that were just steps away.

Along with finding links to the past in places, I found them in people too. I met the son of Raleigh's first black mayor who is a community servant and leader himself, a couple who passed out water at the March on Washington in 1963, and the son and daughter-in-law of one of the founders of a well-known local black printing company. Their lives were testimonies to the heritage around me everywhere.

As I got to know more about the landmarks and people that connected to African American history, my interest in my family's history grew. My granddad was born in Leaksville (Eden), North Carolina. Would living in Raleigh bring me closer to my roots? The State Library of North Carolina held my answer. A book there, *The Cooleemee Plantation and Its People*, included mention of an enslaved man named Ivory, my great-great-great-grandfather. In another part of the library, I saw the death certificate for his son, my great-great-grandfather Peter Hairston, who owned land and built a life in Rockingham County. That discovery sent me on an odyssey to learn more and connect with branches of my family tree that included cousins who live in Wake County.

My fascination with history started in childhood. I was the kid who loved sitting next to Grandma on the porch glider listening to stories of the times before I was born. I was the one who trailed Granddaddy around the garden hoping to hear one of his memories. I was the shadow who followed Mom asking her to tell me about what life was like when she was my age. Living in Raleigh has heightened my interest in the past and in people's stories of their lives. But here, I no longer just listen to the stories. I have become a teller, too.

As I have fun with my kids around the city, I find teachable moments all around. When I took my little girl to the Richard B. Harrison Library for the Mollie Huston Lee doll tea party, I used that as an opportunity to tell her about Mrs. Lee being the library founder and first African American librarian in Wake County. We talked about how blessed we are to be able to go into a library created to make sure the African American community was served.

At the annual African American Cultural Celebration held in January at the North Carolina Museum of History, my son and daughter love doing crafts and listening to the soulful music. But I make sure they know it's more than a Saturday outing. The event salutes the contributions of African Americans to Raleigh and the state. We've met musicians and craftspeople whose art has been passed down for generations. We've seen dramatic renditions of important moments in history. We've listened to storytellers share an oral tradition with roots in Africa that lives on today.

Last year, we took the scenic route home from the celebration and drove down Oberlin Road. I told my kids about a settlement of freedpeople who once called that area home. They created a community, called

Oberlin Village, with houses, churches, and businesses. A minister founded Latta University there in 1892 to educate the descendants of people who had been enslaved.

"Really?" my daughter said. "That's cool."

I think so too. I'm grateful that pieces of the past are around us every day. I've lived in Raleigh for more than a decade and feel like it is part of me. Here, my kids know that they too came from somebody. They are part of a legacy.

KELLY STARLING LYONS is a children's book author whose mission is to transform moments, memories, and history into stories of discovery. Her books include *Hope's Gift* (a 2013 SIBA Okra Pick); *Tea Cakes for Tosh* (a 2012 SIBA Okra Pick); *NEATE: Eddie's Ordeal*; *One Million Men and Me*; and *Ellen's Broom* (a Junior Library Guild selection and North Carolina Children's Book-award nominee), inspired by a document she saw while researching family history.

Views in Fiction

Of Innocence and Wild Irish Rose

SHEILA SMITH McKOY

RALEIGH WAS AT THE CULTURAL CROSSROADS in 1942. Jazz and blues had found their way all over the area because of WLLE, "Willie" radio. You had to listen to WLLE while the sun shone because the FCC and the city fathers had decreed that the station go off the air at sundown "for the common good." Those who lived their lives on the three-quarter time beat of the blues knew better. They knew the fear that the South had of black folk after dark. But after the jazz and blues set with the sun, all of Raleigh's folk—black, white, and indiscriminate—listened to the same music after dark. Then, B.B. King gave way to the mourning licks and long-ings of Hank Williams, where country married the blues. It was on one of those nights when the longing lyrics of Patsy Cline and Connie Francis had taken the night that Drake Lucas made his winding way home.

In the dying scarlet of the western sky, Drake walked slowly down New Bern Avenue, stumbling his way from Sky Lee's place, a rooming house turned liquor house and juke joint that entertained East Raleigh's labor force on most weekends. Drake was still wearing his work clothes, caked here and there with bits of the concrete that he finished for Chey-enne Concrete Company every day except Sunday. He paused beside the road to try to wipe the cobwebs from his face, but since the webs were woven by the Richard's Wild Irish Rose wine in his back pocket, the task was fruitless.

He took out the sweet-smelling bottle to drink a little more, standing still in the road and swaying as he sipped. Even so, he did not want to go home and face his wife drunk again. So much so that the closer he got to his red-trimmed dollar-down house just off of New Bern Avenue, between Elm and Oak, the more he realized that Richard was his best friend. He drained the last drop from the bottle when he stepped on the porch. Just before he made sure she would have heard his brogan boots on the porch, he started singing some Connie Francis.

"Who's slorry now?" he slurred along with the Connie Francis song playing in his head as she was accompanied by the screeching door. When he didn't hear his wife's usual, angry greeting, he sang some more.

"Who's slorry now? Who's heart is aching for breakin' each vow? Who's slad and blue, who's crying too? Jes' like I cried over you. . . ."

"Shut the hell up, Drake. Aint you got no sense? Coming in my house drunk. And where is your money? Don't bother looking at me like you crazy, either. Just give it to me now so I wont have to ask you no more." Drake looked at his wife of twelve years, knowing what would come next, still hoping that he was somehow drunk enough that it would not matter.

"Whatchu mean, Brenda?" he said, but as usual, when he and Richard had been spending quality time together, he said "Brenna," instead. "You know I always brang my money home to you on Friday. Here it is." He staggered a bit as he stuck his hand in the front pocket of his bibbed overalls. He slowly pulled a handful of crumpled bills and made his weekly offering to his wife. She grabbed for the money, launching several of the crumpled bills aloft. They floated downward, in slow motion, as if their hard times lay wrinkled with them on the floor. Brenda was dressed in a red outfit with smears of red across her lips and cheeks. His eyes were a bit hazy from the wine he had drank, but he could still see she wasn't dressed for him. He felt the warmth of the coal stove that sat in the center of the front room as he watched his wife gathering her things to leave. Going where, he never, in twelve years of Friday nights, had had the nerve to ask.

"Right to the en' jus' like a friend. I tried to warn you somehow," Drake sang, scenting the air with the sweet and sour flowers of Wild Irish Rose with his every breath.

"You going out, Brenna? Baby?" he finally got out just before she got out the door.

"Yeah, Drake. I'm going out. How did you guess? And Junior aint ate yet." And she walked out the door. A slight smile played at his lips when he realized that she hadn't even looked back at him before she left. He walked to the front window and watched her step out to the street just as the black Cadillac came to a stop. Like she did every Friday night, she took his heart and his money to Lee Rennick. He had long ago stopped trying to think of plausible reasons why he never tried to stop her. Why every time he brought home his pay, the same money that Lee Rennick paid him to smooth his concrete, that Lee just didn't keep it and give it directly to Brenda himself.

Drake crossed the hardwood floor that had not been waxed in several years and he sat down heavily on the overstuffed brown chair that had been designated as "his." He took a deep breath when he remembered that the Wild Irish Rose was all gone, and the sadness came so quickly down that he was almost caught by surprise. He was about to let the sadness all out, to try to see if the feeling of it felt any deeper than holding it aloft, when Junior called him back to his dulling pain.

The boy looked like an angel standing in the doorway to his room. He was the brightest child Drake had ever known. At three, he could already count to a hundred and he could read. His eyes were big, light brown, and heavily lashed. He was beautiful in the creamy sort of way that marked him as an innocent, as a boy who looked nothing like the man he called Daddy.

"Daddy, I don't feel good," the boy said, knowing not to even ask for his mother.

Drake stood up strong in front of his son, not wanting Junior to see that he was less than the man he felt he should be.

"Well, then, let Daddy see what he can do to make you feel better, Little Junior."

He picked up the boy, holding him close. His forehead felt hot against Drake's chest, so he settled him in his chair and wrapped him in a blanket. He went into the kitchen and sliced an onion. Then, he brought the half onion back to the living room, and placed it where his boy could breathe on it to break his fever, just like his mother used to do for him.

"Daddy is gonna fix you some soup, Junior, and then we are going to play some. Okay, son?"

Junior smiled a saddening smile, but his eyes were bright and happy. That smile was what made Drake go to work every day and come home to a wife who knew nothing about love. This child was his true heart. As he made the chicken broth, simmering some sliced spring onions and carrots, he sang some Nat King Cole pleading, "Baby, Baby, Baby, what is the matter with you. . . ." He left the pot with its softly boiling bubbles, and went to gather his child into his arms, intent on sitting him in his lap and teaching him some Patsy Cline while the soup finished. With any luck, he thought, the boy's fever would break and they would wake up in the morning with their make-believe mother and wife back home.

When he saw Junior, wrapped in his favorite blanket, unbreathing, he tried not to think that he was gone. Drake heard his boots thundering swiftly across the floor toward Junior, even though he knew there was no place to run from death. When Drake touched him, his skin had already lost its fevered heat. Junior was clammy and cold. And he was gone. His and Brenda's and Lee Rennick's baby boy was gone.

Drake gathered the child in his arms, and rocked him for a while. But when there was no more need to find solace in the empty shell of his child, he gently picked him up and walked out of the house. He left the soup to burn on the stove, not bothering to close the door behind him. He walked back down New Bern Avenue, amazed that the moon was still

180

so bright when Junior was gone. Every few moments he would marvel at the shadows playing across his child's face, sometimes shaped like leaves and limbs, sometimes like a memory.

He heard the strands of some mournful song when he got to Sky Lee's place where he knew his best friend Richard would be waiting. He started to go in. But about half way there, he decided that he would follow his heart and take Junior to the water. He would go to the place where the magic of the moon lit the rippling water, where he could trade his fractured heart for the life of his child. His child. Not Brenda's, not Lee Rennick's, but his child.

Drake turned at Tarboro Road, heading for Oakwood, where the cemetery was halved by an ever-widening brook and where the Confederate dead still rested in segregated sleep. At the bend of the creek, where the water flows slowly downstream, he laid Junior down beyond the reach of mortal arms, where spirit and water and the moon waited to take him.

SHEILA SMITH McKOY is director of the African American Cultural Center at North Carolina State University, where she is also on the English department faculty and director of the Africana studies program. A poet, literary critic, and fiction writer, she has written for such publications as *African American Women Writers 1910–1940, Callaloo,* and *Journal of Ethnic American Literature.* She is the editor of *Obsidian: Literature in the African Diaspora.* Her book, *When Whites Riot,* received critical acclaim in the U.S. and South Africa.

The Devil Himself

G.D. GEARINO

THEIR NAMES WERE BILL AND ZEB. They had known each other for all of their twelve years, and had in fact been born on the same day in the same town, that town of course being Raleigh. They lived a mile or so due east of the capitol building, near the spot where the state agricultural exposition and fair was held in its early years, until the war caused grown-ups to declare that fairs and such were a distraction from the more important matters at hand, those matters specifically being the defeat of the invading Union army.

But on a warm spring day in 1865, not only was the Union army not banished from the Southern homeland, it was hunkered down just outside Raleigh proper, having settled itself atop and around Dix Hill. The presence of those soldiers had caused Bill to propose early on that same spring day that he and Zeb undertake an expedition.

"Let's go see the Yankees," Bill said.

Zeb, always the more cautious of the two, saw a problem with that plan right away. "That's crazy," he said. "They'll kill us."

It was a well-founded fear. The Union army, after all, was exclusively populated with murderers, thieves, scoundrels, and knaves. The inmates of every prison and jail in the North had been clad in blue, given a gun, and sent South to prey on decent people. When they arrived in any town, its women were violated, its men were executed, and infants were speared with bayonets and held aloft as the marauders scampered with joy. Everyone knew these things were true.

Bill scoffed. "They'll have to catch us first. We're just gonna look, anyway. Besides, they do anything to us, our fellas are gonna whip 'em."

"If that was true, they'd have whipped 'em by now already," Zeb said. "Momma says the war's over."

"That's why we better go now. They'll be leaving soon, and we'll miss our chance," Bill said.

Zeb made one last attempt to derail this foolishness. "I have to take a bunch of eggs over to the Yarborough House today. I can't do nothing."

Zeb's mother kept chickens in a pen behind the house and made money by supplying eggs to a few eating establishments along Fayetteville Street, the city's main boulevard that stretched from the lawn of the capitol building six blocks south to the governor's palace, whereupon it veered off in the direction of Dix Hill, where the very same baby-stabbing Yankees that Bill proposed to visit were now camped. Zeb knew his mistake as soon as the words left his mouth.

"That's perfect!" Bill said. "I'll help you deliver the eggs, and then we'll go see the Yankees. They ain't but just a little further away. Nobody'll even know we've been gone."

The boys went to the back of Zeb's house, where they found the eggs packed for delivery in a wooden crate lined with rags sitting on a table near the chicken pen. A few of the chickens were outside the pen, having either somehow flapped their way over the wire — they were panicky creatures, as Zeb knew, and in moments of hysteria could achieve a right impressive amount of altitude — or been let out by Zeb's mother for the sake of insect control in the yard. Whatever the case, they made contented clucks as they pecked their way about the ground.

Zeb's mother was suddenly in the doorway. "What are you two up to?" she asked. The woman had a nose for foolishness.

"Nothing," Zeb said. "We were just getting ready to take the eggs."

"We? They ain't so heavy that it requires both of you," she said.

Bill considered that a little diplomacy might be in order. "We're going to take turns carrying 'em, to make sure none get broke," he said.

Zeb's mother regarded them skeptically for a moment, then issued one instruction. "Don't dawdle," she said before turning back inside the house.

The boys headed west on Tarboro Road, which led straight to the capitol grounds, and twenty minutes later they stopped on the lawn to rest a bit before heading to the Yarborough. "I thought we were going to take turns," Zeb said.

"We are. I'll carry 'em the rest of the way," Bill replied.

"It ain't but four more blocks," Zeb said. "I can see the dang place from here."

Bill ignored him. "What do you reckon we ought to do when we see the Yankees? I wonder how many of them there will be. I bet it's a thousand."

"First one I see, I'm turning around and going home. They's killers."

Bill stood and picked up the crate as promised. "I ain't scared. Let's go."

They walked down Fayetteville Street, which was oddly quiet. There were only a few wagons out, and a small scattering of people on the sidewalk and visible through store windows. A peculiar lassitude hung over the city, and there was a sense of menace in the air, too. It caused Zeb to recall a similar feeling one stormish day a few years prior when the rain suddenly stopped, all the animals went quiet, and his father stood outside with his head cocked, not really looking at the dark, ugly clouds that scudded by immediately overhead but instead seeming to try to peer through them. Zeb was frightened that day, and frightened again when he heard someone later say that a terrible wind had struck nearby and destroyed buildings and killed people.

Even Bill was affected by the strangeness of the morning. "Where is everybody?" he whispered.

"I don't know," Zeb whispered back. "I say we drop off these eggs and get straight home."

Bill didn't argue that time, apparently having lost his appetite for Yankee-hunting. They stepped more quickly toward the Yarborough, covering the last block almost at a run. Zeb was nervous about the eggs getting jostled, but not so much so that he suggested they slow down. They arrived at the hotel within minutes, scrambling through the back entrance closest to the kitchen where Bill heaved the crate onto a sideboard.

The commotion of their arrival attracted the attention of the kitchen manager. "I don't pay for broken eggs," he said. "How many you got?"

"Thirty," Zeb said.

"We'll see," the man said, and proceeded to count them. He grunted when he finished, seeming to be disappointed to find none had shattered, and wordlessly wrote out a receipt that he handed to Zeb.

The boys retraced their steps toward the front of the hotel and Fayetteville Street, with Bill chattering nervously the whole way, weighing out loud the merits of returning home versus a rekindling of their reconnaissance of Dix Hill. As they got to the street, Bill's chatter suddenly stopped. "Oh, Lordy," he said, eyes wide with alarm as he looked over Zeb's shoulder.

Zeb turned and saw four Union soldiers on horseback not twenty yards away, cantering toward them. They didn't need to go in search of Yankees. The Yankees had found them.

"We better hide!" Zeb said. There was a huge rhododendron at the corner of the hotel, with untrimmed branches hanging low to the ground. The boys scrambled underneath the branches, crawling on their stomachs to get close to the trunk. They heard the riders draw closer, and to their horror they saw, just beyond the lowest branches, horse hooves approach the rhododendron and then stop. For a few moments there were only the sounds of the horses nickering, until one of the Yankees said, "They might be spies."

"Could be," said another.

"Major, what do we do with spies?" the first Yankee asked.

"Generally, we hang 'em, sir."

This time, the first Yankee addressed the rhododendron directly. "Boys, show yourselves."

Bill and Zeb crawled out from underneath the branches and stood. The four Yankees sat knee to knee on their horses. One of them, an older fellow with tired eyes and a close, gingery beard, said, "Are you spying on us?"

Bill, for all his earlier bravado, seemed close to tears, so it was left to Zeb to answer. "No, sir, we weren't. Please don't hang us."

"Son, you need not worry about that," the Yankee said. "I don't believe either of you have a gift for spying, frankly. I take it you live around here."

"Yes, sir," Zeb said, pointing east behind the hotel. "Back yonder a little ways."

"And I imagine you took a notion to see some soldiers, is that right?" the Yankee asked. Bill and Zeb both nodded.

"How old are you two?" he said.

"Twelve," Zeb answered.

"Well, I was a twelve-year-old boy myself at one point, and I imagine I would have wanted to see some soldiers, too," the Yankee said.

One of the other Union riders spoke up. "General, there's a train waiting to take us to Durham Station."

The older fellow ignored him. "Where are your fathers?" he asked the boys.

"In the war," Zeb said.

The Yankee looked at Bill. "Yours too?" Bill nodded.

"I'm sure they served well, but the war's over," the Yankee said, having apparently consulted with Zeb's mother on this matter. "They'll be home soon, God willing."

"Sir, we must go," the other rider said.

The four Yankees turned their horses and resumed their journey, but they had only gotten steps away when the older one wheeled his horse and returned to where Bill and Zeb still stood. He leaned out of the saddle and offered his hand to each boy in turn. "I like a young man with spirit," he said.

The men cantered up the street and were soon out of sight. Just two days later came the news that the war, truly and officially, was concluded. Bill and Zeb told everyone they knew about their encounter with the Yankees, told everyone that they had shaken hands with the devil himself. Not a single soul believed them.

187

G.D. GEARINO, a Georgia native, is a thirty-five year veteran of the newspaper and magazine industry. He is also the author of four novels, including *What the Deaf-Mute Heard*, the film version of which ranks as the most-watched Hallmark Hall of Fame feature in history. Gearino has lived in Raleigh for twenty years and expects to die there, later rather than sooner.

Hungry

ANGELA DAVIS-GARDNER

I MAY BE AN OLD WOMAN, ma'am, but this big fine house on Blount Street is mine, I have the deed to it and I can also prove that I was reared here by my Mama, she was sickly, and my Papa who was a railroad man and after they died I lived here for a right good while with my husband Floyd.

The house looks like a wedding cake, some say. Would you take exception to that? At our wedding we had a big cake full of sweetmeats.

We never did have children, in case you're wondering. I hungered for at least one, but Floyd held back.

I sure do like cake frosting, vanilla especially. I don't even mind if it's from a can. I used to get my mixes and frostings and what have you down at the Winn-Dixie on Person Street where I walked with the baby buggy that I bought anyway. It's hard to come by frosting now that the store is gone. I don't have any store at all to walk to, no ma'am I don't.

No ma'am I'm fine, I'm not one to complain, I don't need as much as I used to. I'm the kind of old woman who dried up instead of spread and I've always had a dainty figure. Floyd appreciated that but he liked to tease me too. One day he said I was too small to live in such a big house by myself and I said well I reckon you better move in given this view of the situation and help me fill it up. So he did and that was the beginning of not much at all.

Now Floyd's gone, Mama's gone, the Moores who used to live over on Oakwood, they're gone, down in the cemetery, Judge Clark's widow on Polk Street who used to come calling. I don't know my neighbors anymore not one says pea turkey and no one comes to call except when you came around the corner just now and surprised me in the garden.

I seen you before with that dog on a leash when I went for a walk down Bloodworth one time and I hope you're not planning to turn me in, ma'am. I was just looking at what people laid out on the curb. You wouldn't believe what kind of things these young people set out. Boxes of cereal and grits, brand new and the other day a stick of butter once I found a army medal and a tiny ring about yay big it just fit on my little finger, and some other diamonds, a tiara, see, and bread, donuts, pizza pie, Floyd used to love his pizza, a little child's toy of a clown that spins around I put it in the nursery and a Christmas stocking and some hose that didn't have but one hole in them and a storybook with pictures in it and window sash with some trim on it that used to be in my room I guess somebody stole it and my curtains. Now why don't you investigate that instead of picking on a poor old woman?

Wait, ma'am, don't go let me pet your little dog we could sit in the swing for a spell and have some of Mama's fudge and I could show you the article about me that came out in the paper where I didn't tell them because I don't like to complain I wasn't raised that way but I could confide it to you if you just come back I could tell you you're a nice lady and this is the truth on my Mama's honor.

I stay so hungry.

ANGELA DAVIS-GARDNER wrote her first novel, *Felice*, while living at 312 Oakwood Avenue. She has since published three other novels, most recently *Butterfly's Child*, and numerous stories and essays. A distinguished professor emerita at North Carolina State University, she has won many awards for her teaching and writing.

The Carousel at Pullen Park

An excerpt from Bootlegger's Daughter

MARGARET MARON

AUTHOR'S NOTE: In this passage from *Bootlegger's Daughter*, lawyer and judicial candidate Deborah Knott yields to the pleas for help from Denn McCloy, who's running from the law because he's afraid he's going to be arrested for the murder of his boyfriend.

AGAINST MY BETTER JUDGMENT, I finally agreed to meet him at Pullen Park, a venerable Raleigh landmark a mile or so west of the Capitol.

When I hung up the phone, the sun was shining brightly, so I'd driven out of Dobbs with nothing warmer on my arms than the thin beige cardigan that matched my tailored beige slacks. Even before I reached Garner, I'd passed through two heavy downpours and the temperature had dropped considerably.

Definitely not my idea of merry-go-round weather.

The latest cloudburst had dwindled into a fine mist as I drove into the nearly empty parking lot beside Pullen Park, and when I got out to lock my car, I shivered in the damp chill.

I followed the sound of an old-fashioned calliope past banks of rain-drenched roses and day lilies, past hydrangeas so heavy with water that their blue flower heads bent to the ground till I came to a round wooden structure bounded by wire netting and a waist-high plank wall.

Raleigh's carousel is a true jewel, a beautifully restored turn-of-the-century Dentzel. Purists think it ought to be in a museum and are horrified that the city keeps letting children clamber around on the fanciful menagerie, kicking their heels against those enameled flanks to spur them on year after year. Personally, I applaud the city's thinking: the animals are much happier out here than they'd ever be in a museum.

But how like Denn to choose a place like this for a rendezvous. He knew perfectly well he should turn himself in to Sheriff Bo Poole and try to hire himself a Perry Mason. Instead, he wanted to do the carousel scene from *Strangers on a Train*. With all this rain turning on and off like somebody fixing a water spigot, I had the feeling it was going to be more Larry, Curly, and Moe than Farley Granger and Robert Walker.

Oh, well, at least it wasn't the observation deck of the Empire State Building. (Yes, I'm a video junkie.)

Actually, if the day had continued as hot and sunny as it began, the park might have made a good place to meet, crowded as it usually was with kids of all ages. Here in the rain, though, there were only a half-dozen children waiting to ride, one accompanied by what looked like a part-time father, the others divided between two young mothers and an older woman.

Obeying Denn's now-ridiculous instructions, I bought a ticket and watched the beautifully tooled, overhead iron cranks raise and lower the animals as the whole wonderful contraption moved round and round with a measured grace almost lost in our computerized world. Back then, people were less fastidious about hiding the gears and crankshafts of their machinery. In fact, it must have been solid and comforting to see, proof and promise that man could solve almost every problem with sturdy engineering.

The loopy swirling music of the restored Wurlitzer band organ made me think of Teddy Roosevelt, trolley cars, and white eyelet dresses tied with pink and blue sashes.

The round wooden platform slowed to a stop and I went straight to the very same animal that had been my favorite as a child: a proud gray cat with a green saddle blanket and a goldfish in his mouth. Back then it was the only animal I trusted to go up and down in proper merry-go-round fashion.

Farm kids don't get taken to city parks all that often, and I was almost too big for the carousel before I finally figured out how to tell in advance whether the steed I'd chosen would prance or remain frozen in place. Till then, if my cat was already taken and I was forced to choose another animal, it was all pure chance. I would sit apprehensively in the alien wooden saddle till the music started, waiting to see if I'd been lucky. Dismayed resignation if my tiger or reindeer kept its feet on the ground, but, oh, the sheer bliss if it slowly surged upward as the menagerie gained momentum!

The first ride came to an end and I bought a second ticket. The muscular young man who manually shifted the mechanical gears in the center acted like he thought I'd come straight over to the cat near him because I wanted to flirt. Since it was a slow day, he gave us a longer ride. The children and the two mothers were delighted, the father and grandmother exchanged disapproving frowns. I didn't feel like explaining about childhood trust and checked my watch wondering where Denn was.

"Don't look like he's coming," said the operator as the second ride finally ended.

I just smiled enigmatically and walked off into the mist like Lauren Bacall, past the fish-feeding station, over the bridge, under the willows, around the lake, and back past the swimming pool—all deserted except for the ducks that paddled along in case I had a loaf of bread with me. If Denn McCloy was anywhere in the park, I couldn't see him.

A gray Ford pickup had materialized near one of the service areas, but before I got my hopes up, I saw that it sported one of those silver-gray permanent licenses issued to state-owned vehicles.

The skies turned dirty gray again; the mist became distinct drops. The hell with it, I thought. It was bad enough I hadn't called [the sheriff's department] the minute I hung up from talking with Denn. Why should I stand out here and get drenched to the bone playing out his games?

I rounded the full-sized, 1940s-style caboose parked beside the miniature train track and was heading for my car when I heard, "Psst! Deborah!"

"Denn?"

"Shh!"

I looked up and saw him gesturing dramatically from one of the caboose windows. Damned if it wasn't going to be *Strangers on a Train* after all.

Native Tar Heel **MARGARET MARON** has published twenty-eight mystery novels, including *Three-Day Town, Southern Discomfort,* and, most recently, *The Buzzard Table.* She is the recipient of numerous awards including the Agatha, Edgar, Anthony, and Macavity awards. In 2008, she received the North Carolina Award for Literature, and in 2013, Mystery Writers of America named her a Grand Master, its highest award.

Ladies of the Marble Hearth

HILLARY HEBERT

THE MORNING OF THE 420th meeting of the Marble Hearth Book Club, Eunice, Mama's friend, clutches my arm as I dash out of the rain and into Mama's kitchen. "Honey, your Mama's in a stew. The ceiling's about to fall in the living room." Mama's in the hall, pale, stricken, eighty-three, in her snap-front housecoat. In two hours her living room will be sizzling with female gentry.

"We won't let another ceiling fall in this house, Mama. Not today." I pat her arm. "Mama, you've got bed head." I chide her when she gets overwrought. "Go work on your hair, and I'll see about the ceiling."

I drape my raincoat over the shower rod in the hall bath. My silk blouse is dry, but I can feel the little sweaty film that betrays even the best-concealed panic.

From an ominous overhead fissure, water is collecting in big, glassy drops then spilling onto Mama's plum velvet chair. I inhale slowly and organize my thoughts. Blow-dry the chair, arrange the flowers, wash the lettuce, carve the turkey, slice the tomato aspic, make coffee. But first, we need a roofer.

Mama's house was built in 1932. She's lived in it since the day it was finished. She prefers death over relocation. So I do what I can to help her live independently. Before she learned to use her cordless phone, I'd rush over any time she didn't answer in ten rings, burst in like a paramedic at a fire, and find her sitting under her hair dryer reading *Southern Living*.

I think of Mama and her house as two grand dames on a precipice. Less than a year ago her bedroom ceiling collapsed, spewing rubble and dust and plaster chunks the way an earthquake does. A big crack had snaked across her ceiling, and she called my school about ten minutes after I'd left for the airport. She got her new roof, but I don't think she ever forgave me for being out of town.

"This leak's not so bad, Mama." I am less optimistic than I sound, however. Since I started taking antidepressants three months ago, I've discovered that I can make my voice sound cheery. Part of my mind engages with the cheery sound. The other part steps forward and, in hushed tones, narrates the truth.

She calls to me from her bedroom. "It's a crime the way they treat old people in old houses. I shouldn't have paid in full for that new roof."

The blow-dryer I gave Mama years ago is still in its box. "Here, Eunice. See what you can do about the damp spot on the chair." Mama hands me her telephone book with the roofer's number inside the back cover.

"I'm calling about a roof you replaced last summer for my mother, Mrs. Charles Worthington. This is an emergency." After a pause, I am connected to a crackling male voice that fades in and out. "Bob Davis probably handled that job, and he's left the company. Best I can do is check it tomorrow." I tell him it's leaking where a book club is meeting in two hours and that an endangered breed is at risk. He chuckles, and I wait through suspenseful static. Finally he says he'll swing by and have a look.

"Relax, Mama," I say, rubbing her broad, tense back. "He's coming to fix it." She takes a folded tissue from her pocket and dabs her upper lip. "Honey, I don't know what I'd do without you."

It's something I've thought about, but Lord, now that she's eighty-three, a widow, and I'm her only child, how could I leave? Since my divorce four years ago, I've had a nice apartment three miles away. Once we discussed sharing a home, but she stopped cold when I mentioned blending my futon with her mahogany reproductions. Neither of us has mentioned it since.

"Oh, Mama, you'd be so clever you'd surprise yourself."

I clear the counter so I can carve the turkey I baked while I was here Saturday. Before I went home, I put dishes, crystal, and silver out on the dining room table, so mostly I just have food to deal with today. Food and—if my mental harness comes loose—that pesky issue of why I'm here in the first place. All day Saturday, while I was basting the turkey, cleaning the chandelier, scrubbing the bathtub, this nagging feeling haunted me: I'm supposed to be somewhere else. I took the wrong bus. I'm not a middle-aged, divorced, elementary school art teacher who pays for a sub on the day of her mother's book club. I'm really an architect living in a SoHo loft with gleaming wood floors and a five-thousand dollar chair. Just one magnificent chair. Something German. I meet my friends in cafes.

Eunice comes into the kitchen and reports that the velvet chair is almost dry. I check my watch and begin to choreograph out loud: "Wine as the ladies chat and get settled; then the dinner plates with coffee cups; I'll walk the dessert tray around." While Eunice is putting away the hair dryer, I give Mama a stack of fancy paper napkins to fold.

Mama's never been the type to knit, quilt, or crochet. She cooks and feeds. And she longs for me to assume these traditions of Southern hospitality. The day after Christmas she started planning today's April luncheon. When I suggested paper plates and chicken salad from the deli, she stiffened and glared at me as if I had taken the name Emily Post in vain. "Honey," she said, closing her arms around her big chest, "chances are, this is the last luncheon I'll ever give." She stared me down with her cloudy blue eyes. "It'll be my swan song."

Compromise is hard for Mama; she misses rolling out her Italian cutwork linens and seating everyone at tables. For her, this luncheon will be a scaled-down affair. But, however minimally, it still satisfies the home economics directives she gave her students in the Forties: something substantial—turkey; something light and leafy—iceberg lettuce; a vegetable—tomato aspic; something sweet or tart—baked fruit; and something salty or crunchy—Combo pretzels, which mark her an up-to-date, modern hostess. Juxtaposed to tastes and textures will be shape and color of foods. Played against the floral English Sunnyvale china pattern will be white bread, red aspic, green lettuce, gold Combos, and the jewel-toned baked fruit medley of apricots, cherries, plums, pineapple, peaches, and blueberries. Geometric variety will be satisfied by square aspic, triangular sandwiches, cylindrical Combos, and the amorphous meandering of the baked fruit.

Mama hands me the napkins, each perfectly folded. "That roofing man was hard to deal with last summer. Said they'd be through in two days, but he let that crew horse around for almost three weeks before they finished. I had to talk to him about punctuality."

"It's a different roofing man this time, Mama. The one you dealt with left the company."

"He deserved to be fired. You weren't here. You don't know what a time I had."

But of course I know. Every detail. And my therapist knows, too. When Mama called last summer to tell me about her ceiling, it was the first time in five years I'd left town with a man. Forty-two years old, and I was still skewing details for Mama: "Oh it's the usual bunch from school going." I ask myself how a professional woman who is entrusted with young lives can cave in like wet sand at the thought of her mother's disapproval. Anyway, when the roofer got to Mama's late that afternoon, he assured her the ceiling wouldn't fall before his crew could come on Monday. All evening Mama worried over the dark, menacing rupture while I, jetting toward St. Thomas with Peter, was just starting to feel life in my forsaken female circuitry.

About ten o'clock that night Mama knew either one half of her ceiling was getting lower than the other or she was hallucinating. By then, I was sitting under a freshly stuccoed old St. Thomas ceiling with Peter, bare feet propped on a little glass-top table, admiring my painted toenails. While we ate smoked almonds and drank Scotch, Mama was covering her bedroom furniture in old blankets and bedspreads, and fixing herself a place to sleep in her den. About midnight she was awakened by a noise like a plane ripping through her roof, crashing into her bedroom. When she called Econo Roofers the next morning, she got an answering machine and an emergency 24-hour number that was no longer in service.

Thinking about the roofing ordeal—and Peter—makes me grumpy.

"Eunice, Mama, you girls need to save your energy for later. Go rest up." If I've got to work in the kitchen, I prefer to do it alone.

But in Mama's kitchen, I'm never alone. Her voice carries from her bedroom. "Use the Henckel knife to cut the aspic so you won't tear the edges. Don't open the Combos yet so they'll stay crunchy. And Eloise, honey, you know to make the sandwiches so every bite of bread has turkey with it. And leave the baked fruit in the refrigerator until the very last minute. That juice *has to stay thick.*"

I haven't seen Peter for six months now. I'd met him when he created a safety campaign using the artwork of one of my students. His marriage had come unglued, and his wife had designs on his former boss. Once when we were crewing on a friend's boat, he put his arm on my shoulder and said I was his midlife course correction. But in the end he settled for his not-quite-ex-wife, who's a ringleader or potentate or something in the Junior League.

I'm surprised when I spot the Pyrex dish of baked fruit out on the counter, behind the paper towels. It takes a second before I realize what's going on. Unless the fruit stays cold, the juice will run on the plates and turn the bread pink, or maybe orange. And that would suit Eunice just fine. I put it back into the refrigerator.

Like Mama, Eunice descends from a line of anointed Southern women who were granted a higher understanding of domestic propriety. When it comes to preparing a luncheon, along with that higher understanding goes an unspoken covenant: There will be one voice (known henceforth as "the hostess") that chooses the menu, selects linens and serving pieces, and either arranges or directs the arrangement of flowers. There is no harmony sweeter or more forthcoming than a cadre of Southern women preparing a luncheon as long as there is only one hostess. Everyone else is a helper.

Last summer, Eunice's daughter, Mary Louise, pushed Eunice into moving into a retirement community. So Eunice's grand hostessing days are over. She's been trying to convince Mama it's time to give up her house, too. Of course, outwardly, Eunice and Mama disdain any form of competitiveness for its unladylike connotation.

Among their circle of friends, Mama and Eunice have always been the arbiters of taste and decorum. Throughout my childhood, mothers of the bride called Mama to ask everything from how to tie ribbons around table skirts to where to put the tray of netted rice bags. Such questions were deserving of jurisprudence, and Mama waved me away violently if I made noise while she was on the phone. Almost as urgent were the calls pertaining to food and matters of culinary presentation. If Mama had said you were supposed to drink soup from a pickle fork, I think certain ladies would have poked holes in their tongues trying.

When I was young, it was fun knowing that other mothers called Mama for advice. Some of the mothers waited to see if Mama would let me do things, like car date, before they gave their daughters permission. But what had given me status in grade school caused trouble later on. Several girls, including Mary Louise, blamed me when they couldn't car date. Still, Mama gloried in her sphere of influence right up to the day I ran away and got married.

Mama maintained her position as culinary and nuptial priestess, though, despite my little life-wrecking mishap of a marriage. Shortly after my stunt, as Mama called it, Eunice and Mama began a yearlong planning odyssey for Mary Louise's mammoth church wedding. Eunice was so happy she glowed in the dark. I helped Mama tie almost a thousand netted rice bags and gained fifteen pounds.

When my marriage ended I hauled my broken self back to Mama's. She supported me for over a year after the man I'd loved since high school—the same man she never trusted and begged me not to marry—turned as mean as she said he would.

Walking back and forth arranging chairs, I hear Mama and Eunice fussing in the kitchen. Mama says the baked fruit, thickened with cornstarch, and presumably chilled, will hold itself together and not wander over to the sandwiches. Eunice insists the risk of runaway juice is too great. Plus, Eunice reminds her, the tomato aspic could melt if it touches the hot coffee cups.

"If you serve the fruit in compotes, you won't have to worry," Eunice says, pleased to provide the solution.

"My compotes are too high, and besides, the coffee cups have to go on the plates, too. Compotes will tip over," Mama says.

"Then put the fruit in plastic cups. The little squatty kind."

"Eunice, I won't have plastic cups resting on my fine china."

"Then you're going to have a mess. Fruit syrup dripping on somebody's clothes. They say Ultrasuede is washable, but who's going to put a $500 suit in the washer!"

"Eloise, honey, will you get me my little pills?" Mama picks up a recipe card and fans herself. "Wait," she says, when I hand her the digitalis. "We're going to call the Party Shop to see if they have the small plastic cups." I am stunned that Mama acquiesced on the cups so quickly. Satisfied now, Eunice busies herself arranging squares of aspic on ruffled lettuce. Mama follows me to the hall phone and dials while I read her the number. I can see Eunice from the hall; she pauses to listen as Mama asks about the cups.

Eunice is puttering again when Mama and I come back into the kitchen. Mama shakes her head. "No luck." Eunice props her hand on her hip and gives a loud sigh.

"Look, Eunice," I say, "I'm sure we can keep that fruit from getting runny. It's back in the refrigerator getting all nice and firm."

We're almost down to an hour and I'm getting uneasy about the roofing man. I'm worried about the ladies with plates on their laps in the living room. All those shaking hands pinching little teacup handles, polite sips of coffee over laps full of tomato aspic and sticky baked fruit.

I set out the cups. "It's sixteen we need, right, Mama?"

"Sixteen. Unless Eleanor had to go back to her doctor about her gallbladder. Did I tell you her daughter and son-in-law both took off from work to go talk to her doctor? They said if he didn't know what to do for her they'd find another doctor who did, and boy let me tell you, he got on the phone and called in another ... "

I turn on the water to wash a cup that still has lipstick on the rim. If that roofing man doesn't get here soon, I'm thinking about calling the members and canceling. If this were anything but Mama's book club, I would have cancelled it an hour ago.

The Marble Hearth Book Club boomeranged into existence in the fall of 1956 about an hour after Mary Lee Williams telephoned Eunice to tell her that neither of them had been invited to join the Book Ends Club. Mama couldn't join the new Marble Hearth then because she had the full care of my ailing grandmother. But after Granny's funeral several years later, Eunice called one day to say it was time for Mama to join the Marble Hearth. Mama went out that afternoon and bought a biography of Eleanor Roosevelt. She put one of those *This book belongs to* ... stickers in the front and took it to the March meeting of the Marble Hearth Book Club. She became member number twenty, and then they voted to close the membership forever.

After Eunice got her new Louis XIV dining room furniture, she proposed that they start serving lunch instead of just refreshments. What Eunice couldn't do in the kitchen she made up for with her new furnishings. With its leaves in place, Eunice's new table could seat twenty. Mama was irritated because our table wasn't as large as Eunice's and she had to supplement with two card tables in the living room. But Mama could show the club what real entertaining was all about. Before I was born, Mama was head of the home economics department at East Carolina College. Every spring her seniors prepared a banquet for the college administrators and prominent alumni. A flat soufflé or runny meringue was a threat to graduation.

In half an hour, Mama's living room will start filling up with grandmothers and great-grandmothers in silk dresses and pastel suits. Unless I pull chairs out into the middle of the room and expose a patch where an electrical outlet shorted, some of them will sit beneath a four-foot square of ceiling that resembles the surface of oatmeal.

"What did you and Eunice decide to do about serving the baked fruit?" I ask as I fasten the hook on Mama's dress.

"We're not having any plastic cups," Mama huffs. "Anybody with kitty brains knows you don't put plastic cups on the same plate with Castleton china." I brush loose silver hairs from her shoulders then go back into the kitchen.

I'm filling the silver sugar bowl when a truck pulls into the driveway. Econo Roofers, finally.

"Mama, I'll take care of the roofing man so you and Eunice can finish getting the food ready."

I lead him to the trapdoor inside an upstairs closet. He's hefty and tall, six feet or more, yet he folds himself as easily as a dancer. He pulls out his flashlight to search the seams of each rafter. As we talk about the age of the house, his voice softens a little, almost reverently. His hands are big, nails groomed. He says things like "architectural integrity" and "pride in work-manship." He rests his hand on a joist then looks up at me, "Did you ever read Tracy Kidder's book, *House*?"

Well, it so happens I read it last summer. I want to stay and talk about the book, but it's almost curtain time. I go back downstairs and line up the flatware and napkins and run hot water into the silver pitcher. I heat a kettle for tea and go into the dining room to get the dessert trays.

The rain has stopped, but wet leaves and twigs have made the walkway dangerous for elderly guests. I tell Eunice I'm going to sweep the porch and steps.

When I get back inside, Eunice says Mama's heart is acting up again and so she's lying down. Eunice has put everything on the plates except the baked fruit. I spot it in the Pyrex dish, resting on the hot burner where I'd heated the kettle.

Before I can do anything about it, I have to open the door to let the roof-ing man back in. "There's a hole in the flashing," he says. "That's how the water's getting in. It won't take long to fix, but I'll need to get back upstairs to check it when I finish," he explains, with a quick smile. I'm guessing he's well over six feet tall. His tan Dockers are a little snug; his blue oxford cloth shirt is pleasantly rumpled. His boots are those of a Maine woods-man. "About half the ceiling needs replacing," he says, looking up at the bubbly plaster, "but it's not going to fall on anybody today. Do you need help moving chairs or anything?"

"Oh, no. We're okay. Just do whatever you need to do to keep the rain out and the ceiling intact," I say, looking at my watch. Any minute now the house will be teeming with Ultrasuede, baroque pearls, Estée Lauder, sup-port stockings, and heavy diamonds on brown-spotted hands. He seems nice enough, but I want him to take his big boots and exit so the Marble Hearth Book Club can meet in here one last time. So Mama's swans can sing.

He puts on his big yellow poncho and goes back on the roof. The smell of Mama's hair spray drifts out into the hall. Eunice is putting tiny sprigs of parsley on top of each turkey sandwich as Mama walks into the dining room. I stand in the doorway for a moment trying to think if everything is set: The cream and sugar are on the silver tray. I fill a crystal bowl with Sweet'n Low. Maybe these are the kinds of things Peter's wife worries about all the time.

Eunice reaches to the back of the stove and begins spooning runny baked fruit onto the plates.

"Eunice!" The minute I speak her name the doorbell rings. Mama's arranging the books and the borrowers' list beside the cut flowers. "Will you get the door, honey?"

She must have tipped the vase. Water's dripping on the rug. I dash to the bathroom and pull a hand towel off the rack. I give it to her and go to the front door.

"Miss Daisy Moore—I haven't seen you since book club last year!" I hug her tiny frame, which is curling toward the ground. She was my music teacher, a fact both of us kindly ignore. Behind her is Myrtle Tucker with her long, skinny neck and that tight bun still knotted at her collar. She didn't learn to drive until she was sixty-five. She was visiting Mama one day when I was little and Mama was making me practice the proper way to introduce people. I came in from school with my girlfriend, Alice. *Alice,* I said, *this is my mother's friend, Miss Turtle Mucker.*

I grab the hand towel from Mama on my way to the coat closet. Mama is standing tall. Her fingernails are freshly polished, her downy-soft hair waves gently around her face. She is majestic in her size 18 royal-blue silk dress. People used to say Mama looked just like Kate Smith. That's how Mama looks to me right now. God bless America. The swans are singing.

I rush back into the kitchen to see what Eunice is up to, but I don't see her. All the plates are served and the Pyrex dish is soaking in the sink.

Eunice comes out of the bathroom. Her tinted brown hair is combed back from her face; her soft, peachy skin is radiant against her teal linen dress.

The living room fills up with pastel colors and voices that shake like Katherine Hepburn's. Mama offers her guests the glasses I filled with Chablis. Miss Daisy Moore settles into the velvet chair beneath the square of oatmeal ceiling. Through the top corner of the window behind her, I see brown boots on the ladder. Maybe the boots would like to talk about Kidder's *House* in a coffee shop near the college.

Mama and Eunice circulate and chat while the ladies of the Marble Hearth sip wine and update the borrowed-books list. The roofing man comes back in and goes around through the kitchen and upstairs. I hear him tapping, but I don't think anyone else notices. I keep an eye on the damp outline above Daisy. A powdery mist drifts down from overhead.

I bring out all the plates and then come around with the coffee. When I pass the tray of cream and sugar I notice that the fruit is soaking just a tiny bit into the corners of the bread. I don't see any melted squares of aspic.

I duck into the kitchen and crunch a few Combos and line the silver tray with paper doilies. I arrange concentric rings of lemon tarts, cinnamon squares, date bars, and ladyfingers. Mama likes a focal point in every arrangement, so I dash outside and break off a few holly leaves and nandina berries. I wash the greenery quickly, then center the colorful little cluster on the tray. I circle the living room heating everyone's coffee, then go back for the dessert tray. When I lower the sweets in front of Alma Highsmith, she pauses, perhaps stirred by an echo of some medical admonition. Then she smiles and plucks a tart and a ladyfinger. I am on my way toward Marjorie Biggs when a spider scoots out from under a holly leaf onto a tart. Smoothly as a magician, I graze the fluted crust, palm the little bugger, and hide it under the tray. Mama pats my arm as I go by and tells me the tray is lovely.

Back in the kitchen, I stuff a few more Combos into my mouth and clear the sink to make space for the dirty dishes. I'm squirting Joy into the sink when I hear Alma call the meeting to order. I turn on the hot water and close the kitchen door. I walk back to the sink, watching bubbles rise like a head on beer. I put the silver and crystal into the hot suds. I wash and rinse each piece. I'm not going to tell Mama how Eunice melted the fruit; and I'm certainly not going to tell Eunice that Mama was holding down the switch hook when we called the Party Shop.

When the roofer returns, I tell him Mama's roof should be covered under warranty. He marks an invoice *No/Charge*, then hands it to me. I think again about the Tracy Kidder book, and I want to say something, but a little undertow sucks the words right down my throat.

"Eloise is in here, she's doing dishes." I hear Mama's voice from the hall. She and Alma come in, beaming. Alma wants to hug me before she leaves.

"Your Mama is so lucky to have a daughter who can entertain just the way she always has." I smile and thank Alma, squeezing her bony hand. I help her smooth the collar on her rose trench coat. The roofer seems to be waiting for something. He just stands there, watching.

A Raleigh native, **HILLARY HEBERT** writes both Southern fiction and corporate marketing copy, savoring similar derring-dos in both worlds. Her stories have appeared in literary magazines and in *New Stories from the South*.

George Delivers the Goods

An excerpt from Good News from Outer Space

JOHN KESSEL

AUTHOR'S NOTE: *Good News from Outer Space* is an apocalyptic satire about the end of the world, fusing the predictions of the Second Coming as understood by millennial Christians reading the Revelation of John with reports of intervening aliens as understood by UFO believers. In this chapter, Raleigh has been taken over by desperate pilgrims from all over the nation, led by media preacher the Reverend Jimmy-Don Gilray, who believe that Christ will come again at midnight on December 31, landing in a mile-square spaceship in nearby Research Triangle Park. George Eberhardt, a non-believer, is trying to avoid the disaster and save his estranged wife, Lucy, who demands that he perform a task for her in order to win her compliance.

Thursday, December 30

GEORGE AWOKE STIFF, cold, and hungry on the floor of the university lounge, to discover that overnight the courtyard outside the windows had been blanketed by another layer of snow. He stared dumbly, blinking. A sparrow landed on the branch of an oak, shaking off a flurry of powder that drifted to the unmarred ground. In a trance, he picked his way through the forty or fifty others sleeping on the floor to the doors at the end of the lounge. He stepped outside. Although the sun had not yet risen, there was enough light, gray and indirect, to see everything clearly. It was as beautiful a morning as he had ever seen. The air was still: no traffic, no sirens, no planes or people. His breath came out in billows. The cold woke his senses. He felt strong.

After a few minutes he went back inside. Others were stirring, checking their shopping bags full of clothes and their purses full of useless money. He had been wrong to worry about running out of cash. In Zion there was nothing to buy, and the few things worth buying could not be bought.

George hobbled back to his corner. The calculator, pistol, and extra ammunition clip were still there. Despite Zion's calls for pilgrims to arrive bearing weapons, George had not been fool enough to think the border guards would let him keep the gun. It had taken him a week of planning to find the right spot, well away from the roads, where he could avoid both the National Guard laying siege to the Reverend's utopia and Zion's own border militia. He did not suppose himself to be the only pilgrim in Zion in possession of a weapon unknown to the city's rulers; he probably wasn't even the only one there with the intention of killing the Reverend, but he was going to be the one who succeeded.

People were up now, heading for the bathrooms near the dead elevator, rolling up their blankets and sleeping bags. The director of the lounge-turned-barracks, a flustered woman with the sad eyes of a basset hound, got up on a chair and tried to get their attention. "Praise God!" she called.

"Amen," responded a few of the people.

"Let us pray." She led them in a fervent, somewhat erratic prayer thanking God for their lives, the snow, and the television, and asking Him to keep them one more day until His arrival. George stared at the tattered cuffs of the man in front of him.

After it was over the woman surprised them. From the cupboard in the abandoned snack bar she produced a coffee urn and a box filled with vending machine pastry. The sugar coatings of the sweet rolls were crystallized from age. The woman assigned two of the female pilgrims to cut the pastries into pieces small enough so that everyone would get one.

She loaded the urn with water from the tap, poured a single pack of ground coffee into the brewing basket, and plugged it in.

The pilgrims' good cheer was undeniable. George was moved. He knew that some of these people had hounded nonbelievers out of the city. Others had done worse. Yet their fellow-feeling was genuine. It was a mystery, perhaps *the* mystery.

While George sat, staring out the window at the snow and sipping his ounce of coffee, a man next to him spoke. "Where you from?"

The man was in his mid-fifties. He wore a plaid jacket over at least a couple of shirts; an orange hunter's cap pulled low over his forehead, green rubber work boots with yellow soles. He was freshly shaved. A bit of bloody brown paper towel was stuck to a cut in the dimple on his chin.

"New York," said George.

"I'm from Texas," the man said. He stuck out his hand. "John Field."

"George . . . Lowell."

"George, when did you get on to God's team?"

"In April."

"A latecomer. But praise God, not too late!"

"How about you?"

John Field leaned forward, forearms on his knees. "I can tell you the exact minute: December 11, 1997, 11:45 p.m. Waco, Texas. I was watching the TV, feeling as bad as I ever felt in my natural life. My wife had just left me, I was out of a job for seven months, drunker than a skunk, and I hadn't had but one bath in maybe three weeks. I was flipping through the cable channels, climbing up through the stations into the high numbers that didn't have nothing on them, just snow and hissing. You can tell just what a sorry piece of work I was at that time, George, when I tell you that suited me just fine. I liked going up through the numbers, higher and higher, getting back nothing but noise. It was like I was climbing up through the layers of my brain, and there was nothing there but noise, too. I was piss-eyed drunk, and piss-eyed mean. If you'd come in that room just then I would of spit in your eye."

"What happened?"

"As I was watching I came across a station that had a picture on it, and the picture was the face of Our Lord Jesus Christ Himself. I can even remember the channel—channel 777. Jesus said to me, 'John, I want you to stop acting like a rodeo clown. Clean up your act. Pick up this room. Take a bath. Find yourself some honest work. When Tolene comes back, you get down on your knees and beg that good woman to forgive you. The End Time is coming. You hear me?'

"I thought it was some kind of movie. I didn't say nothing. But Jesus keeps looking at me and then he says, 'Wake up, John!' and he points his finger at me. A pink laser beam shoots out from his finger and hits me right between the eyes. A blast of cold fills my skull. All that noise up there goes away as if he pulled a plug. It about melted me right there in my chair. I was dazzled. I knew that I was all right, and when the last day came, I was going to sit by His side. I must of passed out, because when I woke up the TV was full of snow again. But I wasn't. I remembered it all just like it happened, and there was a fire burning in my heart."

John Field looked across the snowy courtyard. "It burns there still, George. I got the greatest gift you can get, the gift of grace. Tolene did come back. She told me she was halfway to her momma's house in San Antonio when she decided she would give me one last chance. I asked her what time that would of happened, and she told me about a quarter to twelve. I got down on my knees and kissed her feet. I promised her I would never give her a day's worry again."

A woman came over and put her hand on Field's shoulder. "John. We have to get ready." She smiled at George. "Hello," she said.

"Hello," said George. To John Field he said, "Thanks for the testimony."

"We had better get ready," said Tolene.

210

"See you later." Field took his wife's hand and they went over to a group of people who were getting into costumes. John Field sat on one of the low tables, stiff as a bride being dressed for her wedding, while Tolene Field took off his hat and pressed down upon his head a crown of thorns. She helped him off with his jacket and, one by one, the layers of shirts, to reveal his back, crisscrossed with suppurating wounds. He did not flinch. Around the room others were donning burlap robes. Two men struggled to get into a large papier-maché costume that had once been a pantomime horse but which now represented the ten-horned Beast of the Apocalypse.

George felt very alone. A Mighty Fortress is Our God. The people took up their whips, their signs, their crosses, and set out for the penulti-mate rally.

After they had gone George got to work on his own costume. He fash-ioned a burlap robe from some bedding. Out in the courtyard he scraped the snow from the remains of a bonfire and blackened his face with ashes. He teased his straggly hair into further wildness. Using the knife they had cut the pastry with, he began cutting a six-foot staff from a dead dogwood. His breath steamed in the cold air and despite his exertion he was freez-ing. He told himself he was a crazy religious fanatic. He tried mumbling to himself. It was easy. As he worked he heard cheers from the street. A couple of young men ran across the quadrangle, kicking up clouds of powder. They saw him hacking at the tree, laughed and ran on.

He got the staff into shape, adjusted the pistol in his belt beneath the robe, made sure the calculator was still in his pocket, and examined his reflection in the lounge windows. Quite respectable. He set off for Cap-ital Square.

The streets were filled with people. Most headed downtown, but a sig-nificant number were going the other way, starting the long trek to the Landing Pad. George fell in step with a man who was talking to himself and a woman carrying a sign that had a taped-on photo of a silvery UFO and the slogan *Fish Cannot Carry Guns*. George clutched her coat and peered into her face. "Have you seen Him?" he demanded. The man came close—it was the Lord's Prayer he was chanting—but made no move to stop George.

"No," the woman said. She pulled free. George let them go. No one cared about George's performance: In the City of Saints, he did not even rate a second glance.

In front of the Brownstone Hotel a group of pilgrims was building a cross of snow. Children broke from the effort to throw snowballs at each other, their laughter edged with hysteria. A boy dashed by, wearing a woman's sweater and a winter cap with the earflaps pulled down. There was some tumult up the street. A block away, in front of what had once been a pricey hotel, a crowd spilled across the trampled snow. From the hotel balcony a man harangued them through a bullhorn. Scuffles broke out between listeners supporting and attacking the speaker.

Something about the man with the bullhorn was familiar.

George pressed closer through the mob until he could get a good look. Men in fatigues stood by the rail on either side of the man, automatic rifles held at the ready, and scanned the mass of people filling the street between the hotel and the burned-out shell of the Green Party headquarters. The speaker wore a blue swallowtail coat and American-flag pants. His white hair hung over his collar and the point of his Van Dyck beard stuck out beneath the bell of the bullhorn. It was Uncle Sam.

"Millions now living are already Dead!" Uncle Sam shouted. "From the neck up, anyway." His cackle was turned mechanical by the horn. "Following around these preachers. You're Americans! The Constitution guarantees you freedom from religion. But you've pissed it all away!"

That drew angry shouts, but among the crowd were some who yelled support. "It's time for us to act like free people and throw off the shackles of medieval superstition! This Reverend Gill-face interprets the Bible for you and you suck it up like pigs at the trough. Well, I'm here to tell you to grow up! The man who does the interpreting is the man who has the power! You give up your power to him just because he tells you he can read better than you can? I don't know whether to laugh or spit!

"You know St. Paul? Well, St. Paul says, 'Though I speak with the tongues of men and of angels, and have not love, I am become as sounding brass, or a tinkling cymbal.' You've been deafened by the biggest sounding brass in America! I wonder if you can hear anymore! Can you hear me? Are you listening? Are your brains working?"

Curses and cheers. George got shoved and almost lost his balance. He was directly in front of the balcony.

"Your Reverend Jimmy-Don's voice booms like a church bell: loud because it's hollow. He has force but no authority. Noise but no signal. Power but no —"

Someone threw a brick, which narrowly missed Uncle Sam and whanged off the wall behind him. The guards raised their rifles and searched through the crowd. Someone screamed and the mob surged forward. Uncle Sam pointed into the seething mass. "Deconstruct that fella!"

A couple of supporters attacked the brick thrower. Others came to his defense, and a melee broke out. The gunmen on the balcony could not get a clear shot. Uncle Sam started to clamber over the balcony to drop into the parking lot, but before George could see what happened next he was knocked down by someone hurtling into him from behind. He took a knee in his temple, grabbed hold of someone's coat to keep from getting trampled. His vision swam. He staggered to his feet. The rally had become a riot. George struggled forward, was shoved through a row of junipers against the wall of the building. He sidled away from the thick of the fighting.

From downtown came a siren. A police truck, beacons flashing, pressed into the crowd. Garbled commands roared from its roof loudspeaker, and a bunch of men jumped out of the back wielding baseball bats. The crack of a rifle from the balcony above George was answered by fire from the militia, and the body of one of Uncle Sam's riflemen flopped over the rail to land a yard in front of George among the bushes. George didn't wait to see what happened next: He slid around the corner of the building and, still clutching his staff, hurried to the alley between the houses on the side street. Behind him he heard a cheer.

Several others, like George, were hightailing it through the backyards. A middle-aged man shouted out a back door, "What's happening?"

"That Uncle Sam! He started a riot!"

"He's crazy," another man said. "The Antichrist." The man looked George up and down.

"I'm the Wandering Jew," George said. He threw his staff over a chain-link fence and clambered over into a snow-covered garden. His hands were numb. Panting, he hurried up the next street away from the fighting. Numbers of people spilled into the side streets, but the sound of gunfire had been replaced by more cheering. George had no interest in finding out who had won, but he would not have put much of a bet on Uncle Sam's chances.

As George crossed a bridge over some railroad tracks a pickup full of militia shot by him up the snow-rutted street, horn blaring. A couple of refugees from the fight skidded into the gutter to keep from getting run down. George bent to help a woman in an expensive coat. Her companion, a red-faced man in a threadbare blazer, brushed snow from the knees of his pants. The pickup spun out as it took the turn at the end of the street and disappeared on the way out of town.

"Attack on Highway 54," the man said.

"The heathen armies," the woman said. "The president's made a deal with the Japs. They're going to attack!"

"You're crazy," an angry man said. "It's a holy revolution in Greensboro! Christians have risen up and are marching to break the blockade."

"They're trying to get the power plant from us," a man on the other side of the bridge shouted. "The nucular plant — cut off the power and freeze us out."

"It's the Advance Landing Modules." Another man had crept up beside them and whispered in George's ear. "The ALM's are distributing manna. We should get to the Landing Pad."

George stared at the people. "It's the Second Coming," George said. "And I've got to meet Him this time." He hobbled to the end of the bridge and slid down the embankment, through snow-covered kudzu vines to the railroad tracks. As the people above watched, he started down the roadbed toward the center of the city.

By the time he reached Capital Square he was exhausted. The militia ringing the old capitol building looked tense. For three days George had been hearing rumors of a massacre of the Saints' militia in the west. One of the commanders had had a vision of invincibility. He would march his men outside the lines; the guns of the National Guardsmen would throw flowers. He and his men were slaughtered before they'd gone a hundred yards. Their bodies still lay there. Some believed that when the Savior came on Friday night they'd rise up, truly invulnerable, and complete their sortie, devastating the army of the Antichrist.

The militia at the Capitol, however, didn't look reassured by that expectation. Behind the barbed wire and metal-stake barricade encircling the statehouse, young men in fatigues clutched rifles and mugs of steaming coffee. They stood stiffly around trash-barrel fires, expecting to be shot by some sniper or raptured out of their bodies at any second. Only the statehouse and its surrounding park of memorials stood indifferent, as if waiting for this, too, to pass. Across the snow-covered lawn, a man with a chainsaw cut a dead oak into firewood. The snarl of the saw bit sharply through the cold air.

Uncomfortably aware of the snouts of the machine guns, George approached the south entrance of the square. The young man posted there trained his rifle on him. He would not make eye contact. The name strip across his breast pocket was blank.

"They haven't told you your new name yet?" George asked.

The boy looked confused. "Who are you supposed to be?"

"I'm the Wandering Jew."

"Well, wander away from here."

"I can't do that."

The young man poked the M-16 at George's belly. "Go away."

A couple of other men came toward them from behind the barricade. "He can't come until I find Him," said George. "It's prophesied. I'm the Jew who denied Him."

One of the advancing men heard George. "Do tell," he said. "We've been expecting you."

George forced himself to be bold. "You could give me a better reception, then. It's hard traveling for a two-thousand-year-old man."

"It's hard even on the younger ones, pilgrim."

"It's no thanks to your sort that I got here in time. Two millennia of suffering for me and my people! Every corrupt politician, whenever he got himself into trouble, just had to point at a Jew to get the heat off his back."

"It's the truth," the third militiaman said.

"Let me tell you, pal," George said. "I'm not going to make the same mistake twice. Have you seen Him around?"

The oldest man smiled. "Not yet. Come back tomorrow night."

"How about you let me in now?"

"Why?"

"I want to pray at the foot of the statue."

"What statue?"

"General Washington."

"What's that got to do with Jesus?"

"I believe in all martyrs."

The man looked skeptical. "Okay," he said. He gestured with the barrel of his rifle. "But you try anything funny and you won't last till tomorrow."

They pulled back and let George past the barbed wire.

The statue, surrounded by a short iron picket fence and bracketed by two cannons, stood on a little rise before the south portico. Washington, in a bronze greatcoat, leaned on a walking stick like a country gentleman. George knelt down beside the right-hand cannon. He folded his hands up under his robe and bowed his head. He pulled the calculator from his pocket. He had forced himself not to speculate why Lucy wanted it. Maybe she had arbitrarily picked an absurd task. Maybe she needed to balance her checkbook.

George wondered how she had gotten from South Carolina to Richard's phone. For the hundredth time George pushed back the thought of her being pursued in the dark by who knew what while he ran away. He looked at the statue. To the militia who idly watched him he must look like some devout religionist, some worshipper of the American republic. George supposed that in some ways that was accurate. He believed in America as much as Uncle Sam. He couldn't define exactly what he meant by America, but he knew that he genuinely cared for it. Even though Americans were crazy.

Lucy thought he was crazy, but he'd cared for her, too. His knees were freezing. When he stood, he reached out to the cannon as if to steady himself—it was hardly feigned—and slipped the calculator into its muzzle. The iron felt no colder than his hands. Leaning on his staff, he made his way toward a group of soldiers warming themselves around a fire. A few flakes of snow swirled from the sky to melt in the heat rising from the trash barrel. "Bless, you, my Christian brothers," he said. "Can you spare some food for the Wandering Jew?"

"Ain't got no food," one of them said.

"You aren't really a Jew, are you?" another said.

"Two thousand years of waiting!" George poked the man in the chest. "All because I didn't know the Savior when I saw Him. Don't you make the same mistake! If you see this Reverend of yours, tell him I said so."

A tall man dumped an armload of firewood by the barrel.

"You'd best try the courthouse, old man," he said. His voice was not unfriendly. "They've got some food for the pilgrims, I think. We'll keep our eyes peeled."

"See that you do," said George.

An explosion echoed out of the west. The men's heads jerked up; one climbed up on a sandbag to see better until a corporal pulled him down.

A smudge of black smoke rose against the sky. They pushed George out of the enclosure. He shuffled across the street toward the pedestrian mall.

In front of the courthouse a group of penitents scourged each other with barbed wire between rows of heads on stakes. They chanted and cried. Nearby a man hooked jumper cables to a storage battery, then pressed the claws of the cables to the chest of a naked child lying on a blanket. "Depart from this accursed boy, Satan!" he shouted, while beside him another man stood with his hands at his sides and wept.

There was no food.

JOHN KESSEL, two-time winner of Science Fiction's Nebula Award, is the author of the novels *Good News from Outer Space* and *Corrupting Dr. Nice* and the story collections *The Baum Plan for Financial Independence* and *The Collected Kessel. Good News from Outer Space* has recently been released as an ebook, with a new introduction. He teaches in the creative writing program at North Carolina State University.

About the Cover

The cover illustration for *27 Views of Raleigh* is the work of Chapel Hill writer and artist Daniel Wallace. His illustrations have appeared in many publications, including the *Los Angeles Times, Italian Vanity Fair,* and *Our State Magazine.* He also illustrated the book covers of *27 Views of Hillsborough, 27 Views of Chapel Hill, 27 Views of Asheville,* and *27 Views of Durham,* all published by Eno Publishers. And he illustrated *Papadaddy's Book for New Fathers,* by Clyde Edgerton.

Award-winning Books from Eno Publishers

27 Views of Durham
The Bull City in Prose & Poetry
INTRODUCTION BY STEVE SCHEWEL
$15.95/216 pages

27 Views of Asheville
A Southern Mountain Town in Prose & Poetry
INTRODUCTION BY ROB NEUFELD
$15.95/216 pages

27 Views of Chapel Hill
A Southern University Town in Prose & Poetry
INTRODUCTION BY DANIEL WALLACE
$16.50/240 pages

27 Views of Hillsborough
A Southern Town in Prose & Poetry
INTRODUCTION BY MICHAEL MALONE
$15.95/216 pages
Gold IPPY Book Award, Best Anthology
Gold Eric Hoffer Book Award, Culture

Eno's books are available at your local bookshop and from www.enopublishers.org

Chapel Hill in Plain Sight
Notes from the Other Side of the Tracks
DAPHNE ATHAS
$16.95/246 pages

Undaunted Heart
The True Story of a Southern Belle & a Yankee General
SUZY BARILE
$16.95/238 pages
Silver IPPY Book Award, Best Regional Nonfiction

Brook Trout & the Writing Life
The Intermingling of Fishing & Writing in a Novelist's Life
CRAIG NOVA
$15.95/152 pages

Rain Gardening in the South
Ecologically Designed Gardens for Drought,
Deluge & Everything in Between
HELEN KRAUS & ANNE SPAFFORD
$19.95/144 pages
Gold Book Award, Garden Writers Association
Silver Book Award, Garden Writers Association
Silver Benjamin Franklin Book Award
Honorable Mention, Eric Hoffer Book Award